7 Secrets to Profit From Adversity

Success Against All Odds

The Appleseed Training Co Ltd
587 Clearwater Way
Coquitlam BC, V3C 5W5, Canada

National Library of Canada Cataloguing in Publication Data

Roberts, Joe, 1966-
Seven Secrets to Profit from Adversity: Success Against All Odds
/ Joe Roberts.

ISBN 0-9732482-0-3

1. Success in business. 2. Achievement motivation. 3. Roberts, Joe,
1966- I. Title.
HF5386.R53 2003   650.1   C2003-910111-8

First Printing February 2003

Jacket design by Jonathan Cauri Wamai
Typeset by Pesi Unwalla, Mindware Design Communications
Edited by Arlene Quesnelle and Mandy Cunningham
Proof-reding by Karen Winter   (Just Kidding Karen)

Printed and bound in Canada by Friesens

A Dedication

This book is dedicated to my Mother, Arlene Quesnelle, who fought to give me life twice. Once in the winter of 1966 and again in the summer of 1991.

I love you Mom.

"Joe Roberts' inspiring story is one of determination, courage and overcoming adversity that reminds us of the power of believing that anything is possible. It is testament to the strength of the human spirit and what you can achieve when you set your mind to it."

Rick Hansen
Canada's Man In Motion

"Joe, thank you for your courage and vulnerability to share the details of the dark side of your life in this book so others can have hope! Gratefully I am glad your book doesn't stop there but you continue to give the reader a plethora of strategies and tools to go from just plain survival to success. All who read this book, no matter where they are today in life, will benefit greatly from your life experience and your research. Bravo Joe!"

David Sweet
President & CEO Promise Keepers Canada

"Joe's incredible journey is a testament to human survival, perseverance and success against the odds. By transitioning poverty, addiction and homelessness his story gives us all hope that anything is possible if we have faith and dare to dream."

Daniel Loney
President, Loney Financial

"Joe Roberts is one of those rare individuals that really walks his talk as you can see the evidence in the life he leads. His real life story and this book will make you look hard at what your true possibilities in life are. Stay tuned as I am sure we are going to be hearing much more from this individual who shares immediately usable tools that will forever change your life if you just accept and adapt them."

Stuart Ellis Myers
President, Uniquely Speaking

"Few successful people have experienced the depths that Joe Roberts has and lived. He is a man who knows what it is to be truly "down," and, more importantly, how to "get up." The lessons he learned on the way to getting his life back provide a great strategy for anyone who wishes to reach higher than where they currently are. This is a story of the triumph of faith and the human spirit that will be a blessing to anyone."

Ernie Culley
Pastor, Agape Life Center

Contents

FOREWORD BY
DR. PETER LEGGE

LL.D. (Hon), CSP, CPAE, HoF

Experts say we can't rebound until we know we have reached bottom.

Life is a challenge for all of us but for some, life's challenges are truly monumental and one has to have great courage and faith to be an overcomer.

Joe Roberts is one of those people.

His story is truly compelling – a serious one-time cocaine and heroin addict, homeless and living on the seamy side of Vancouver's streets – his life was all but lost.

But the God that created him had new and different plans for his life. He reached down from heaven and reclaimed the miserable life of Joe Roberts. God showed him a new life full of promise and forgiveness.

This book, **7 Secrets to Profit from Adversity – Success Against All Odds**, can show you God's great compassion and love and His purpose for your life.

> John 10:10
> *I have come that you may have life in all its fullness.*

Joe Robert's story is raw, real, frightening and triumphant. It is a great read about a life lost and reclaimed by God.

ACKNOWLEDGEMENTS

My success today is a reflection of the great people I have met along the way. This book and my life, for that matter, would not have been possible without the help of so many.

I want to thank my partner, Pesi Unwalla, for his support and encouragement in pursuing my dreams. Ever so humbly, Pesi has always been the true value of Mindware Design Communications. I've just been the spokesperson. I want to thank also all the special people on the Mindware team including Aaron Solly, Scott Barratt, Edmund Arceo, Javed Haque and Scott Paton.

To my editors and proofreaders, Mandy Cunningham, Arlene Quesnelle and Karen Winter, thanks for turning my graffiti into a book. To all the friends who supported me including Chandrekha Ramcharan, Gerry Contini, Miles MacDonald, Arne Hassel-Gren, Tom Jones, Lanny Flores, Chris Randles and Greg Harder.

A special thanks to my many mentors who encouraged me to tell my story despite my fears, Ian Selbie, Dan Loney, Peter Legge, Lesra Martin and Rick Hansen.

Thanks to Stuart Ellis Myers, who convinced me that my message was relevant and who would not stop in his relentless nagging to get me moving.

To my spiritual Sherpas, Dan Gowe, Tom Howse, Ernie Culley and Dr. Cal Chambers, who guide me spiritually while holding me accountable to God's plan for my life.

To Toastmasters Vancouver and The Canadian Association of

Professional Speakers (CAPS), who have given me a home to foster my love of speaking.

To my early friends in Ontario, Scott MacLeod, Michael Ballard, and David Sweet. To the staff and support of Loyalist College, including my good friend Bernie Belange, and the whole General Arts faculty, Paul Gaudet, Tom Thorne, Hans Kruger and Brad Baragar.

A special thank you to Terry Scott, from Belleville Vocational Rehabilitation, who saw my potential and took a risk on me.

When life was bad there were many who helped. I could not begin to even put a dent in this list but these are the ones that come to mind. To the Salvation Army, who fed, sheltered and loved me when I was unlovable. To St Paul's Hospital emergency staff who fought to keep me alive when I no longer wanted to live. To The Vancouver Ambulance Services, Vancouver Paramedics, Vancouver Detox, Cordova Detox, Barrie Detox, Royal Victoria Hospital in Barrie Ontario, Toronto Western Hospital, Addiction Research Foundation, University of Toronto Medical Staff, Kingston Detox, and finally, Serenity House Belleville, for giving me a safe haven in those first few shaky months.

To all the friends of Mr. Bill, Dr. Bob and Jimmy K – keep a candle in the window and the coffee pots brewing — there's more on the way.

Lastly, to my precious wife, Jennifer, and our little girl, Sarah, who patiently sacrificed their time so that this book could become real. I love you both very much!

INTRODUCTION

In 1989 I left the streets of Vancouver, B.C. Canada a broken, homeless drug addict. For over 10 years I lived a substandard life then something changed and my life began to get better. This book is a collection of my beliefs, my stories and most of all, my philosophy for successful living. Nothing happens without a dream. In 1989 all I could do was dream and dream I did. I dreamed of a day I would no longer feel the pain and degradation that had been my life. Today I am living proof that nothing is bigger than the spirit to win and reach for a better life. Despite all the obstacles we face, *we can overcome,* and live the life we imagine. We can truly profit from adversity. I learned that life doesn't give us what we deserve — it gives us what we negotiate. My mission with this book is to help you negotiate what you want out of life. My hope is that it moves you, in its own way, in its own time, toward the change you want. They say change happens in an instant, a flash, in a moment. As you read this book may you have many such moments as the God in me touches the God in you.

Blessings,

Joe Roberts
Jan, 16th 2003

1

There is nothing better than adversity. Every defeat, every heartbreak, every loss, contains its own seed, its own lesson on how to improve your performance the next time. – Author unknown

SECRET *1*
The Secret *of* Adversity

Just like every summer on this day, I sat on the edge of the gorge and enjoyed the warm summer breeze. I reflected on the many experiences and years that have shaped my life. This is a special time of year for me. This particular day marks a milestone in my life.

I recently saw a movie that described life as a small collection of very good and very bad days. Today was the anniversary of one of my good days. In fact, it was the anniversary of my best day ever.

My custom is to return to this spot in the woods every year and reflect on my life. It has not always been this good. Some might even say it has been cruel and unfair. But as an optimist, I chose to find the good in life's lessons.

Time alone is precious; I spend it thanking God for who I am today. This silence allows me a few moments to think about how beautiful my life has become. Looking down into the deep ravine I can see for miles from my mountain perch. The sky is beautiful today – not a cloud in sight. It's summer in the Pacific Northwest, clear, warm, magnificent. The air is sweet with wildflowers; I hear the sounds of whiskey jacks and ravens circling the trees above. Off in the distance, I hear the rushing water of a stream cascading down my favorite mountain.

As I had done many times before, I brought with me my rose-colored prayer box. This "Prayer Box" is a simple, yet very effective tool I use in my professional and private life. It lets me gain clarity and direction on many issues. I started using it as a way to get ideas out of my mind and down on paper. I jot down a thought, a prayer, an uncertain feeling and drop it into the box. Periodically, I read the notes inside and amazingly, I always find the fears and feelings of uncertainty placed there, have passed. My prayers somehow answered.

I come to my special spot each year to reflect on my year's goals. Taking out the contents of my prayer box, I see the kind of progress I have made. Although the weather on this particular day was perfect, inside I felt cloudy. I was filled with indecision, fear and uncertainty. The past year had been particularly hard for me. I was going through yet another massive shift in my business life. The projects I wanted to complete were not even started. The commitment to move on this major change came with a tidal wave of fear. I was holding back even though this was my ultimate dream. Was I doing the right thing? Do I have what it takes? Can I move past those who say it can't be done? My anxiety leads to sleepless nights and my first grey hair.

Another glorious year had past, one filled with victory and many happy moments. Yet in my "prayer box" there was turmoil. There were unresolved fears and false beliefs. I closed my box and decided I wasn't going to worry about my troubles anymore. I was going to let them all go and just enjoy the day on the mountain.

Focusing on the spectacular view there on the craggy edge, I looked down into the valley 300 feet below. Beyond the rock cliffs on the other side of the gorge, off in the distance I could see my beloved Vancouver, British Columbia. It's a beautiful city, especially viewed from 3,000 feet up. I saw the massive sport stadiums nestled among the ultra modern skyscrapers, the famous Lions Gate Bridge and the outline of the world-renowned Stanley Park. The setting sun reflected on the towers of glass, as it sank behind the island mountain range. Something in me stirred. I found myself staring at my prayer box. It was an old shoebox that my wife, Jennifer, had at one time covered with gift paper adorned with soft pink roses. Suddenly I found myself compelled to do something so spontaneous and out of character it surprised me.

I picked up the box. Bending my knees I stood up, and I threw it into the air with all my strength. I watched as my box went up into the dusk-colored sky. It went up, up, up, until I no longer could see it. It disappeared out of my view and I remember thinking that I was going mad. Later that night I thought about my box and how it kept going up, up. Must have been an updraft or something. Whatever it was, my box was gone.

I was cold, homeless, penniless, and full of shame. How did my life end up like this? It was a Tuesday, the day before Welfare. As I stood in the lineup at the Salvation Army's Harbor Light, all I could think of was getting something to eat. I hadn't showered in weeks and I smelled of the street. My clothes were scrounged from friends and dumpsters, and my hair was dirty, long and matted. My teeth were yellow, fuzzy and unbrushed. I remember it like it was yesterday. The feelings of worthlessness and degradation were at the forefront of my every thought. At just 22 years old I had become a living failure. Homeless, jobless and dependent on alcohol and drugs to comfort my soul, I had turned to petty crime to survive.

I was dumping my self-pity and pain on my friend, Tony. He, on the other hand, had become comfortable with his plight. "Stop whining," he said, "better fed than dead Fred." I'm eternally grateful I never became comfortable with the down-and-out lifestyle. I'm thankful that my discomfort pushed me to the point of change. I have seen far too many good people lose their way in life, not because of their situation, but because of their acceptance of these circumstances. Tony eventually hung himself. I guess that was his way of dealing with his tormented world. I had a better idea, I was going to get out. I was going to make it.

It would be impossible to write a book about successful living without first telling you about my failure. In 1989 I was a homeless skid row derelict with a PhD in defeat. I spent 10 years of my life on the street fighting to stay alive until one day everything changed.

Success today is so important only because I have experienced the bitter taste of defeat. Failure came at an early age as a result of a series of poor choices. I started using drugs at the tender age of nine. I continued to use alcohol and drugs through my early teens and into my adult life. My recovery began at age twenty-four.

In my 15 years of abuse and self-degradation, there were a series of events that I permitted to happen out of poor decisions. I bought IPO stock to a second rate lifestyle. I paid premium for mediocrity and was given a default return on my investment. It was not until I took responsibility for my actions that my world began to change.

One of my presentations is titled, "One Day to Change Your Life Forever." That day for me was July 26, 1991. The day my life changed forever. I wanted more from life but I was so scared of the unknown. Sadly, I was becoming more and more comfortable with the pain and misery I knew. I was so afraid of change I was willing to endure my current state of hopelessness.

One day something finally stirred in me. Something deep down that said, "no more!" Over the years I've talked with many friends about "hitting bottom," I guess I finally hit mine. I did something that day that was remarkable, considering my mental, physical and emotional condition. I promised myself that life was going to change. There must be a better life out there. Surely I wasn't here only to suffer. I vowed I would make my life count for something, and would break free from my self-imposed imprisonment. I made my own declaration of independence and have spent the rest of my life fighting to stay true to it.

Immediately after my decision, life began to change. I found myself living with others who were on the same road.   We began to share our experiences, our fears and our suffering. Something happened when I shared my life with others who had felt this kind of pain. We began to identify with each other. Not through our individual circumstance, as our lives and paths were very different, but through our feelings, our emotions and mental anguish.

Today, as a professional speaker, I meet people from all walks of life and I have discovered something all people share. Every one of us has had to deal with adversity in our lives. Marriages dissolve, careers change, people get ill, loved ones die, and money is lost. We're all given our share of life to live and no one is exempt from the bumps and bruises. What I have today is a choice in how I will deal with the adversity I face.

I can choose to escape like I did for years or I can face today's challenges head-on. I know that no matter what life throws my way, the first defense I will always have is my choice of attitude. This simple, yet universal concept, is what I live by today. When life's storms come my way, I tell myself that nothing lasts forever, that this too shall pass, and I will be a better person with another experience behind me. I'm a strong believer in Winston Churchill's mantra, "Never, never, never, never, never, never give up!"

I don't presume to know what struggles you face, but I do know that we all have roadblocks. My message is simple. You are infinitely stronger than anything life sends your way. If you put all of your life challenges together in a pile and stood yourself beside them, you would see clearly that you are bigger than the sum of adversity. You are greater than any challenge, holding the power needed to overcome anything and everything life throws your way. If you don't believe me, ask me again. You are strong, you are powerful, and you have the strength and endurance to surpass any and all problems.

Why? Because your life proves it. Your pile of struggles hasn't conquered you yet! You're still here, and your adversity has made you stronger. I'm so thankful I learned life the hard way. I'm so grateful for the adversity and pain that I have faced. My experiences have shaped me into the man I am today. I wouldn't trade that for anything.

If you're in a place today where you are unable to fully buy into this concept, I want you to meet me half way. Believe that I believe. Know that others have been where you are now, going through something that feels like it has no end. Know that you are not walking this road alone, that many others have forged ahead and completed their personal journeys. These people are now your cheering section, waiting to welcome you on the side of victory once you've made it through.

For those of you who have made it, I welcome you home. For those on the journey, I shine my light your way and look forward to seeing you soon.

What challenges in your life have helped to shape your character?
What good lessons have you learned from a tragic life experience?

At the age of 24, I went back to school. As a high school drop out with no real career experience or skills, I was ready to prove myself with study and hard work. There was an advantage being a mature student, I wasn't interested in the social aspects of college. I was there to learn, get my diploma and tackle my dream. This focus helped me to eliminate things that were not going to help me achieve my goals. I also found out that I was a pretty sharp guy. For years I thought I wasn't that bright, but when I applied myself I was astonished with the results.

As my studies progressed I discovered something interesting about life. I felt good when I accomplished something worthwhile; I enjoyed what I used to refer to as "work." I really liked each task and each project at school. I was gaining energy and momentum. With each success I began to feel that I could really do something constructive with my life. As the weeks and months passed, I felt myself growing stronger and each win brought more confidence. I became assured that my goals and dreams were attainable. When days were tough, I was able to remind myself from whence I had come. Even if I stopped progressing at that point, I knew I already had accomplished more than I ever expected or wished for. Having lived the last 10 years in extreme adversity, I knew I could handle anything that college or life could throw my way. I was leveraging my life's experiences and it was working for me. I had learned how to profit from my failure. I knew how to use these experiences to motivate and serve me well, instead of dragging my spirit down.

It was a Tuesday when I graduated. The sun was shining bright on our campus. The air was filled with excitement and I was the second proudest person in that auditorium. The first was my mom. As they called the names, each student paraded across the auditorium stage. My name was called next over the crackled PA system. They said, "Joe Roberts, Business Marketing, DEAN'S LIST!" There was a roar from my little section of the auditorium as my mom and some friends gave me a standing 'O.' What everyone else didn't know was that three years earlier I was living under a bridge as a skid row bum.

After college I decided I needed to look for work in a larger market. I considered Toronto or Vancouver. Toronto was familiar and it definitely had room for me to grow, but there was the whole winter thing. My second choice was Vancouver, the weather was certainly better and of course the winters were milder. You may think I was crazy making my choice based on climate but have you ever been in Ontario in January? Nothing fun about 20 below don't ya' know. I grew up shoveling snow and if I get my way, I'll never have to do it again.

I eventually made the decision to leave the East and make Vancouver my new home. With one more bold decision made, I packed up everything into a U-Haul truck, attached my 1982 Honda Civic and headed west for fame and fortune. I had estimated the amount of fuel needed, which I could put on my gas card. I could sleep in the truck cab to save money on hotels. And when I arrived, I could withdraw enough cash using credit card advances to last me approximately two months. My plan and new life was in motion. I was truly on my way. Life is most exciting when we are in a place of transition. It would seem that most of life is either on our way to something or on our way from something. For me it was both. As I enjoyed my drive across this wonderful country, I was excited and full of enthusiasm. I had dreamed about becoming successful and now my dream was only four days and 3,000 miles away.

As I drove over the bridge connecting Vancouver's Lower Mainland and the Trans Canada highway, I remember feeling overwhelmed with joy at the completion of my journey across Canada. I was so optimistic and filled with energy that I began pounding my horn in jubilation! I knew things were going to be hard. But I was up for the challenge and looked forward to my new adventure. There was no turning back.

One advantage to my move out West was that I had my brother Jeff to lean on for a few days. I pulled into his driveway and parked the U-Haul. Within my first week, I got a lead from my sister-in-law Janine who told me her company, Minolta Canada, was always hiring new salespeople. I called up and got an interview the very next day. Not even unpacked, I crawled inside my U-haul truck to the back where my one suit was boxed. I dragged it out, pressed it as best I could and prepared for my interview.

The next morning I waited nervously before I was escorted into the sales manager's office. The gentleman I was about to meet was Lanny Flores, a man to whom I owe a great debt. He looked me up and down and then asked me a few questions about what I had been doing with myself. The one thing I had learned to do quite creatively, was adjust my resume to account for "lost" time. Lanny asked me all sorts of questions, ones that were irrelevant in my opinion. He asked me about life and family. He asked me what I wanted out of my career and where I wanted to go in the future. I looked him straight in the eye and said: "I want to be the best darn sales representative that I can be for Minolta Canada!"

I'm not sure if it was my determination, enthusiasm or the bad suit I was wearing.
Whatever it was – it worked. Lanny hired me on the spot. He walked me into the General Manager's office and announced that I was Minolta's latest hire. I found out later that there was usually a two-stage interview process before being hired, but because Lanny liked me so much, he had decided to hire me on the spot. I would not disappoint him.

After the interview, I bolted back to my brother's place to tell him the good news. In less than five days I had located an apartment, hooked up my phone and cable, moved into my new pad and landed my first solid sales position. Life was new; life was good and all because of the action taken.

After two weeks of intense training, (the same amount of time it takes to create business cards), I was sent to the mean streets of Vancouver to earn my keep. I initiated my sales career in the downtown core. This was the scariest place for a new sales rep to be. This is where competition was its fiercest. As sales reps ascended in the elevators, their competitors would be descending. They would actually follow their competitor's delivery trucks to find out where the latest machines where being delivered and attempt to upset an active deal. I knew I was in a different league and I was scared.

Each office tower loomed above me, housing thousands of potential new prospects that would reject both me, and my product. I had to find a way to summon the courage to begin "cold-calling." I looked at the first tower and it was too big so I walked a little further down the street. The next building was too small. I continued down the row of office buildings until I was standing facing a vacant lot in Vancouver's notorious east side ghetto. There was old fencing and trash strewn about. There was graffiti and a little shanty village in the back corner of the lot, held together with an old blue tarp and orange pallets. I said to myself, "People on skid row don't buy photocopiers and I ought to know." I lived on skid row for a number of years and not one of my friends, cronies or buddies had ever owned or negotiated the sale of a copier or fax machine. I stood there speechless for a brief moment and then decided that I had to bust a move soon or my whole day would be wasted.

I turned tail and headed for the first building within walking distance. It was a modest 12-story building with business offices on every floor. The elevator moved slowly from floor to floor. I had committed myself to cold call the entire building. The seemingly ancient elevator creaked its way even closer to my destination in professional sales. I felt my stomach flip once and then flip back again. "DING," the elevator opened. I charged out and headed for the end of the long hallway. I swung open the first door I set my eyes on and my life dream became a reality. This was the day I became a professional salesman.

I didn't call on the entire 12 floors that day, but I did make a gallant effort. I gathered about 25 business cards and called it a day. It would later turn out that within 90 days, I would convert and close three sales, from that first group of 25 calls.

I would love to tell you that my wins continued so easily but they didn't. I struggled many days just working up the nerve to sell the product I represented. I suffered from "cold call reluctance" and every call I made was a challenge. There was one time I left an office and on the way out, I heard the guy make fun of my pitch. He was mocking what I had said to the rest of the office. I'm sure he didn't mean to hurt my feelings as much as he did and I don't think he realized that the door was left open for me to hear his mockery. I left the building immediately and quit for the day. I vowed to myself that one day I would become a millionaire and the joke would be on him. Whoever you are and wherever you may be today, I want to thank you sir, for the fuel that pushed me further that day.

Lanny used to joke with me on days I would call in "sick." I just didn't want to cold call. He would say to me, "Do you want to die now or later?" Through his thick Filipino accent, the only thing I heard was, "Do you want to dine out later?" He was a great leader. He knew when to push and when to just be a friend. I wish everyone could have the pleasure of working with a great leader like Lanny. Lanny is from the "old school." He came to Canada in the late 1960s and earned his way to the top of one of Vancouver's largest copier companies. Really, he sold his way to the top. His performance was hard to beat and it was all done with integrity and hard work. No sneaky games for Lanny, he was the real article. I was learning a lot, just by observing how Lanny went about his work.

In the beginning, I had no money to spare. I was busy paying off credit card debts I had accumulated from my move out West. Because of this I bought my clothes second-hand at the Salvation Army. I thought no one would notice but they did. Lanny would buy me lunch, sometimes twice a week. He told me that once I earned my first big paycheck then I could buy lunch. He introduced me to sushi and he also introduced me to a kind of leadership that begins in the heart. Not something well explained in books. He introduced me to three ideas. Most importantly, always be kind. Second, always remember that everything you do should be done for someone else. For example, always buy lunch for the new guy! Today I buy lunch everyday and encourage every sales manager out there to buy your people lunch.

Last but not least, get to know your people and remember to show them how much you appreciate them. I can't tell you who won the World Series in 1995. I can't remember last year's Noble Peace prize winner. I can't even tell you who won an Oscar last year. I can, however, tell you the names of the men and women who have taught and guided me. I remember each teacher and hero that touched my life. Lanny is one of them.

Within a very short time, I mastered my selling skills at Minolta and left to move into a sales management role, selling audio-visual business equipment for an American-based company. It was here I met my future business partner. We connected immediately and I knew our friendship and careers were somehow going to be aligned.

Many years have passed since my faith-driven beginnings with Mindware Design Communications and I am so grateful for what I have been blessed with.

Today, I am married to the most beautiful woman in the world. I am debt-free and hold two honor degrees from college. I made my first million in sales before I was 35 years old. By society's standards, I have all the trappings of success. So how did this all come about? Simple. I learned how to profit from failure. Today, I enjoy a life like no other. I learned how to take my life from skid row to profit from adversity and to become the leader I am today.

The lessons I have learned along my journey I wish to share with you in this book. The ideas are universal and can be applied to any struggle or challenge you may be experiencing. If you have found this book and have experienced challenges in your life, give yourself a break and read the next few pages. My hope is to show you that failure is never final and that **you don't have to be up to look up!**

Have you ever been faced with such a dilemma or problem that you felt there was no solution? Have you ever felt like giving up? Have you ever been faced with something that seemed so much bigger than the resources you have?   I know I have! Everyone I meet and talk with has admitted that at some point in their lives they have faced an obstacle that seemed overwhelming. These same people have admitted that everything did work out fine in the end. For some, it was illness or the death of a loved one. For others, it was their career or a financial situation. For some, it was a family dilemma or domestic concern. Whatever your crisis, there is a solution, even though it is hard to see at times.

In 1991, succeeding in the business world seemed like such an unattainable goal. Today it is my reality. I had every legitimate reason in the world to tell you why I could not succeed. I was a high school drop out, I had no connections, I was unemployable, and I was homeless. There was one voice, however, that I could not silence. It was the still, quiet voice in my heart that said, "YES, YOU CAN!" I could not deny this voice. I tried to shake it and ignore it, but it wouldn't cease until I finally agreed that yes, I really could succeed **if I wanted to.** This choice for success was the beginning of the greatest adventure and set of victories in my life. It was also the beginning of an enormous amount of hard work.

Nothing worth going after in life is easy, especially when you see yourself as an underdog. Many days and nights I wanted to quit. I felt I couldn't go another step. I did, and today I'm glad I did. I also learned that I am not alone in my journey. Many before me have overcome their perceived limitations and succeeded beyond their wildest dreams. Many more will go further than me. I am just a humble journeyman on the road of life. A road with a few extra twists and turns. I just took the long way home.

Another interesting thing I've learned is that tremendous success and glory can often be born of what we perceive as failure. I once had the pleasure of reading about a man in America who was born in a log cabin, experienced poverty as a child, received less than one year of formal education in his life, lost his mother when he was 10, three of his four children died very young, and he had failed at many career attempts. He finally did succeed at something. His name was Abraham

Lincoln. He will always be remembered for accomplishments that followed many earlier setbacks. His failure helped build his character, his resolve and his faith.

What setbacks have you experienced in your life? Do you think they have made you stronger? How have they strengthened your faith? Are they keeping you from living your dreams? Are they worse than Abe's? If they are, then get excited for the glory you will undoubtedly experience in the days to come. Nothing is sweeter than victory over a personal demon. Holding your head up high and saying "YES! I made it through that, and I am stronger for the experience."

What if I told you that your past does not define you at all? What if I told you that every mistake you have made will have no bearing on what your future holds? What if I told you that you could not fail at anything you believe you can achieve? What if your future dreams and hopes, are a reality waiting for you to experience? Well, it's true! I may not have every answer in this book to explain the nature of positive thinking or successful living but I can tell you this, I went from being a street person to a CEO. I transcended a life of degradation, hopelessness and pain to a life of success, privilege and happiness.

I learned that no matter what has happened *from this moment forward, your future is spotless.* Let me say it again because this is the most important idea in this chapter: **"From this moment forward your future is spotless!"** Whatever mistakes or shortcomings you have experienced in your life up until now no longer will need to define where you go from here. For years I let my past define me. Ironically, the title of this very book highlights where I have been. The fact is we can choose to do, be, or experience anything we want in life regardless of what we have done in the past. Ultimately, the one thing no one can take from us is our thoughts, our dreams and goals.

So what's stopping you from really going for it? What's preventing you from breaking out and living your dream? Is it fear? Is it false beliefs? Fear was probably my greatest enemy. I used to worry about everything. I worried about money, rejection, health and a multitude of other issues. I guess that makes me human. I think most people struggle with some kind of apprehension. It would seem that fear is the biggest inhibitor on the road to success.

As a business leader and professional speaker, the last thing I wanted to do was to tell people about my life's failures. These are details I would have liked to keep private. My hesitation almost prevented me from being a speaker. I am so grateful I pushed through my fears. I also recognize that I spend way too much energy worrying about issues that never materialize. I once read that 92% of the things we worry about never happen.

Let me ask you a question. Could you list five major concerns you had on this day exactly one year ago? When this question was posed to me it was hard to come up with a single one. The fact is that most things we worry about are minor in the grand scheme of things. Most of what drives us nuts or worries us does not deserve the kind of attention we give it. Where do you want to focus your attention and energy today, on the problem or on the solution?

Everyday I meet extraordinary people, people like you. People who have gifts, talents and noble goals and dreams. I have been blessed with one of the greatest gifts — the ability to take part in the success of others. To play even a small role and see someone take a risk and make it, is a joy I can't express.

The other side of this is that I also meet many who I know have the resources to achieve success, never manage to get their ideas off the ground. Whether they've wanted to improve their sales or be an entrepreneur, there seems to be something holding them back. I think more folks are as equally afraid of success as they are of failure. I don't know all the factors but have managed to narrow down a few key ideas.

The inspiration I had to change my life came from outside of me. They say that a problem cannot be solved by the mind that created it. Well, I can attest to that. This is why I need other people to set examples for me. People's stories of redemption and triumph stay with me. If they could do it, I could do it. I still feed on this basic idea and sustain hope from others. It is only through the help of others that I have made it this far.

There was one particular man I met in the southwestern United States in my early years of recovery that did just that for me. To this day he is one of my heroes. His name is Reg. He was an incredible example of courage and hope. At the tender age of 18, he made a mistake that would alter his life forever. He was drinking one night and decided to drive his pick-up truck home, despite his drunken state. He tells the story of how he woke up in the hospital two days later and could not remember anything that had happened. He remembers looking down the bed at his feet and seeing only one. Reg had crashed his truck and banged himself up very badly. The accident was so severe his right leg had been amputated. If you knew Reg before the crash, you knew he was an active guy. He played sports, enjoyed skiing and swimming. He loved life and played hard. This was devastating for him. What happened over the next few years is not uncommon, he slipped into depression. He drank heavily and withdrew from the world. In deep despair and wallowing in self-pity, he moved to Denver, Colorado.

On arrival in Denver, he stayed with a guy named Tiny Texas Tom. Funny though, Tiny Texas Tom was from New Jersey. He was 6 foot, 7 inches tall and weighed 300 pounds. He was this larger than life "character" you might expect in a Disney movie. One thing was certain, he had a heart of gold, a surplus of positive energy and he believed in people. Tom saw no limitations or obstacles, only opportunity. As the days went by, the Texan from New Jersey tried to encourage Reg to get active again. He saw beyond Reg's disability and included him in everything. He didn't see Reg as disabled and he tried hard to get Reg to share his view.

One sunny Sunday afternoon they were sitting on the porch looking down their little tree-lined street and Tom said, "Hey Reg, you see that mountain bike at the far end of the porch? I think you can ride that!"

Reg replied, "I hate to break the news to you Tom, but I only have one leg."   At this, Tom erupted into a belly laugh that could be heard in three states. He persisted by going over and picking up the bicycle. He grabbed Reg, who at this point had very little choice in the matter, and sat him on the bike. Reg protested that he could not ride this bicycle because his only foot kept slipping off the low spot on the sprocket cycle. "Don't move," Tom bellowed as he ran into the house. In a moment, he was back with a roll of gray duct tape. Quickly he wrapped Reg's foot securely to the pedal and pushed him on his way.

Reg described what happen next. He glided down the street with the wind in his face and for the first time since his accident, Reg was mobile. He began to weave and feel the motion of the bike and it felt good. There was only one obstacle left to conquer – the stop sign at the end of the street. Needless to say, Reg's first bike ride was not without its bumps and bruises. However, with a few modifications, Reg now was riding his bike all over Denver's city streets. If you saw Reg, you would also see his red mountain bike underneath him.

As time went on, Reg's love for cycling increased. He competed at city and regional levels and won. What was amazing is that he was racing against two-legged competitors and beating their pants off. He recalled to me the day he knew his life had been completely transformed. He was invited to compete in the U.S. National competition hosted in Ohio. The starter's pistol sounded and he felt a surge of energy. Within the first mile of the race, he pulled away from the pack, leaving behind some of the best cyclists in America. By the end of the race, Reg had beaten his closest competitor by more than four minutes. Reg had become the best cyclist the country had ever seen and he did it with just one leg.

After winning the Nationals, Reg was approached by an agent who told him that he had a special gift and that if he didn't train professionally he was a fool. He needed no time to decide. Immediately, with a full sponsorship, Reg began training for the Olympics in Barcelona, Spain.

One particularly cold but crisp sunny fall morning outside of Denver, Reg was climbing along a steep mountain road and passed two other experienced cyclists. As he went by, he overheard the one man say, "Let's go Ernie, I'm not going to let no one-legged guy beat me up this mountain." Reg's competitive spirit kicked in. He smiled and decided to give these bikers a ride they wouldn't soon forget. He sped ahead, never letting the pair behind him get too far away. He was secretly enjoying the labored and exasperated breathing noises coming out of the two stragglers. Of course Reg beat them to the top but what happened next was special. The man who made the ugly comment walked up to Reg and said, "Sir, I want to shake your hand, I've been climbing this mountain for 15 years and I have never climbed as fast as I did chasing you today. You are an inspiration to me."

With tears in his eyes, Reg stood atop this great hill looking over the snow-capped Rocky Mountains that surround Denver, he began to think back to a time in his life when things were bad. Hindsight being 20/20, he now could see clearly that his path in life needed to take this twist in order for him to be molded into the person he is today. He said a little prayer of thanks and continued on his ride.

Reg went on to compete at the Barcelona Olympic Games. He didn't get a Gold Medal, but by then he was already a winner, because he had learned how to profit from adversity. I live my life trying to be more like him each day. Reg is one of my heroes.

God gave me the wonderful gift of adversity. He gave me enormous strength to see me through my experiences. He gave me a way to love and reach people who may struggle in life. He gave me a story that can help young people make better decisions in life. He gave me the gift of succeeding beyond adversity, which allows me to connect with business people on topics of sales, leadership and motivation. He gave me a life filled with pain and sadness, and then showed me the way out. I am so glad I had a hard life!! It's really true. What better way to talk about positive thinking and choosing an attitude of success than to know life from both sides?

I also know that today, my experience on skid row is more of a metaphor than anything for most people. There are days that I still end up on skid row in my mind. It's a place of desperation and fear of the unknown. I know many people whose lives and circumstances have not physically taken them to a ghetto, but mentally and emotionally they have experienced it. Our challenge is to face each day's reality as we search for meaning and purpose.

The fact that I have experienced much pain and adversity in my life is what truly makes me effective today. To omit the greatest failures in my life is to ignore the source of my success. We are molded and shaped by our experiences. Who we are today usually is a direct reflection of our past experiences, but it doesn't have to define our future.

I was a homeless street person living in doorways and under bridges in Vancouver's notorious drug-infested East End. My life was a series of let downs, disappointments, painful experiences, suffering circumstances, and very bad choices. I finally was confronted with an ultimatum. Face the fear, pain and uncertainty of changing the course of my life or face death.

On July 26, 1991, I chose to live. Since that day I have made a conscious choice to live each day. I chose life over death. I chose sobriety over drugs. I chose dreams over nightmares. I chose to make life count, one day at a time. I now choose to share my experience with others in hopes that my wisdom and experience will help to move others closer to their dreams and goals.

I stand proud today and I also stand naked for all to judge. I have combined my story along with a map for successful living. My goal is to fill your mind with the idea that anything is possible from this day forward. That you, yes *you*, can become all you dream and hope to be. All your dreams, aspirations and life goals can be accomplished if you set your mind to it. You can overcome any obstacle, see past any challenge and turn your failures into your greatest assets. Listen closely to what is written next, it is what my success is built on. No matter how bad things may look today, no matter what beliefs you may have about yourself or the world around you, no matter how grand or humble your specific dreams may be, they are possible. Not because I say so. Not because someone told me, but because after enormous personal change in my own life, I am part of the evidence.

What challenges have you had to overcome?

It's the bottom of the ninth, bases are loaded with two out. It's a full count. You're down to the last pitch. Your fans are cheering you on...what's it going to be?

Life begins now. Here and now! What are you going to do?

7 Questions:

1. What are the greatest challenges facing you today?

2. How have they changed your view of the world and life?

3. How will these experiences shape your family, your community, and your career?

4. How can you help yourself and others through your experience?

5. How will you continue to thrive, despite your problem and perceived disadvantage?

6. What do you use to inspire and motivate your success?

7. How can you turn you greatest failure into your greatest asset?

2

"Whether you believe you can do a thing or not, you are right."

Henry Ford

Secret *2*
If it's going *to* be,
it's up to me

Today I believe in people, more than just about anything else. I see greatness and talent in every person I meet. I rejoice in our diverse world. I love to hear about people's dreams, goals and passions. I firmly believe that everyone has a burning desire to do something great. I know from experience that everyone I meet is born with the seeds of greatness. Each one of us has a calling, a path to follow. For some, it is being in the public light. For others, it is quiet and rewarding work. Whatever your passion, today I celebrate it with you. I applaud your interests and goals. I want something for you, not from you. When you succeed, I succeed. As a professional speaker, I am blessed in meeting so many people and in hearing how their lives have been affected. These same people have no idea how they have touched my life. Personal and professional growth as a science has been something that has interested me for a long time. Not just from a technique or methodology perspective, but deeper. From a spiritual realm, I believe there is something that happens to us when we start to understand the greatness we all are born with.

Some time ago, I was channel surfing and came across "The Antique Road Show." This is a program that travels from town to town with a film crew and a group of professional appraisers. They fill an hour-long program talking to local people while appraising their old collectables. The show reminds me of a virtual 20th century garage sale. People bring their old furniture and the appraisers tell a detailed, historical story of the piece, sometimes informing the owner the piece is worth thousands. I find it funny to watch the looks on people's faces when they realize what their old junk is really worth. All the looks are about the same, a combination of surprise and amusement, with a pinch of pride wrapped in there. This one episode I was watching was highlighting the finest moments of the show's history. They were airing a previous episode of a Sotheby's auction in New York City, where a piece of furniture first "discovered" on the show was being sold. As I watched the auction, I was amazed at what I saw. The old table sold for over a half-a-million dollars! The woman who owned the table couldn't believe her fortune and I was moved by the metaphor that came to me.

What moved me was the idea that an old piece of junk now was perceived as being incredibly valuable. I thought about my life in contrast. How at one point I was like that old table. Uncared for, dirty and believed to be worthless. But then something happened. Through the help of other people, my own personal worth and value increased. I also placed no value on my thoughts, my dreams or my goals in life. Today, they are worth more than gold.

I had a friend once ask me if I thought God made junk. I asked what he meant by that. He went further to ask me if I believed God could make a mistake. I thought about it for a moment and said "no." No, I did not believe the creator of the universe could possibly make a mistake. He then asked me why I thought so poorly of what God had created in me.

He said, by not believing in myself and by acting out of low self-esteem, that I was indirectly saying that I did not believe in the God that believed in me. He explained to me that he believed every one of us is divinely created and placed on this planet for a purpose. In God's eyes, each one of us is equal. Each one of us has an infinite value bestowed upon us at birth. Our future is limitless, and our potential much greater than we could imagine. We certainly hold more value than the coffee table that sold for a half-a-million. What is the price of a human life? What is a life worth to the universe?

Next he said something I will never forget. "Joe, what would happen if starting tomorrow everybody on this planet woke up and completely understood their full value and the value of the people around them? What if we really started to live like we were the most valuable resource on earth? What if we began to treat others as such? Would it change how you feel? Would it change how you think? Would it change how you live your life?"

For me it changed everything. I'm not suggesting that some kind of new age consciousness will take place while you are reading this book. But if I can get across one idea it would be that we have value beyond measure. Our lives count for something. Our thoughts, dreams, hopes and values matter. As a member of the human race, your stuff matters!

Why am I so big on this idea? I think it's because this is where I see a lot of people getting stuck. This is where I was stuck for years. Always thinking that it was about the world outside, when it was really about the world inside.

You could have all the opportunities in the world and still fail in life. Look how many times we have seen children of privilege or people of fame crash and burn before our eyes? I used to think that if only I had money, or if only I had connections, then I too could succeed in life. I believed that outside things, people and circumstances determined my fate. I later learned that it has nothing to do with your outside circumstances and everything to do with an inward attitude about one's self and the world around you. I have learned that if you are truly going to make it in life, you need to believe in yourself.

If it's going to be, it's up to me.

For years I felt bad about myself. I'm not sure where it began, but I remember at an early age, I had feelings of low esteem and self worth. I felt different than the other kids. I picked up more than my share of baggage growing up. I learned from my parents, my school and others, but not everything I learned from these people was good. As I grew and matured in high school, I remember getting teased a lot. The world I lived in seemed to confirm my belief that I was less than everybody else. Before I was 16 years old, I contemplated suicide because of these very real feelings of complete worthlessness. I believed the world would be better off without me. I was depressed, apathetic, and full of self-pity. I believed that the world was a cruel place in which to live and that nobody loved me. I started acting in self-destructive ways that further ignited my self-fulfilling prophecy of failure. This pattern repeated in my life for more than 10 years. It led me to a physical, spiritual and emotional bottom. It led me to a life on the streets, filled with misery, addiction and pain. Before my life did a 180-degree switch, I remember having such strong degrading thoughts about myself. I couldn't look in a mirror without a feeling of self-loathing. I certainly couldn't look a "normal" person in the eye when I spoke to them — I would always look down at my shoes.

I know most people I meet cannot identify with these specific circumstances, but I'm sure if we're all honest with ourselves, we would admit to times when we felt a little hopeless or unsure of our personal or professional lives. I think it's only natural to question ourselves, especially when facing change. The danger is when the behavior becomes such that it negatively affects our journey, or path in life. The emotional breakdown of energy that occurs when we stop believing in ourselves is probably the number one reason that many dreams lay dormant. I am so grateful that today the man in the mirror is my friend.

But I still have days when I am about to take a risk and I hear that old familiar voice telling me I'm not worth it, I surely will fail. It reminds me of one of the old episodes of the Flintstones where Fred would talk with Kazoo. Kazoo was this little green Martian that used to appear and disappear on Fred's shoulders with the greeting "Hello dumb dumb." Kazoo was consistently doling out bad advice. Each time Fred listened to Kazoo, he was destined for some form of failure or humiliation. The old tapes I have are somewhat familiar. I hear myself saying things like, "I could never do that," "I'm not smart enough" and other limiting thoughts. What is amazing about this process is that once recognized, it can be dealt with and eliminated on a case-by-case basis. Yes, it's true, I still have limiting thought patterns that stem from a history of living below my potential; however, today, I ask them to leave when they appear. It's like asking unwanted company to leave or better yet, stopping them at the door and not letting them in at all. I have a funny little saying I use when thoughts like this visit me. I say, "Thanks for stopping by, you can stay but I'm leaving."

Today, I no longer stay in long periods of negative thought. I simply have too much to get done to waste my time and energy on this. I'm not suggesting that change is an immediate and overnight thing, but I do recognize that today I can choose what to think. Victor Frankle, in his book, "Man's Search For Meaning," detailed that one of the only remaining freedoms that one has in the face of adversity is the ability to choose one's own thoughts. No matter what life throws your way, you ultimately get to choose how you wish to process this information. No one can tell you how to think. It is with this conviction great leaders have led, and great achievements have been accomplished. Today, by choosing to believe in others and myself, I foster an environment that breeds prosperity, not failure. The epiphany was discovering that true personal success was an inside job.

I used to walk into a room asking the question, "What do these people think about me?" Today, I approach the same room thinking, "What do I think about these people?" There has been a shift, not in the world around me, but in the world inside me. Today, I choose to be positive about life, about who I am, about the general state of affairs. It is only from this place that I can ensure continued personal and professional success. The old way of thinking simply would not serve me well as a leader and CEO in the business world. After all, confidence combined with the ability to communicate, are key leadership qualities.

Need Some Help?

When I was turning my life around, I met a wonderful woman who helped me with an exercise that changed my life. First, she helped me identify some of the core issues that led me to think less of myself. She walked me through a process of forgiving both others and myself. She then pointed to the reason the problem persisted. She told me I was listening to the wrong "radio station." When she first told me this, I thought she was off her rocker. I didn't understand what she meant. She continued to explain to me that emotionally, I only was picking up one kind of frequency – a frequency that affirmed my feelings of low self-worth. Out in the world, I was absorbing only these negative messages and ignoring the positive ones. When someone sent a compliment my way, I quickly would dismiss it as being false information. I had conditioned myself to only hear, sense and absorb information that confirmed my feelings of worthlessness. Her advice was simple and yet it changed my life. She told me to carry a pen and paper with me each day, and record every positive and negative message being sent to me. She told me to search hard for the positive messages, they were there, I just had to find them. What followed the next week was amazing. I began to retune my receiver to pick up on positive messages being sent to me. It started with a smile from a store clerk. Next, it was a pleasant hello from the bus driver. It followed with someone complimenting my new sweater, to a friend telling me they appreciate my honesty. By weeks end, I was a new man. I had learned how to reprogram the data being sent to me and interpret the positive as well as the negative.

This was the beginning of a new foundation for my life. It helped me with my education, my business, my marriage and my family life. Today, through listening, I have redefined who I am and how I think and feel about myself.

The other day I was in traffic and made a mistake. The guy ahead of me yelled out his window that he thought I was an $%*$#@! I thought about this for a minute and began to laugh. How can this guy, with so little information about me, make this kind of statement? He hasn't interviewed my friends, has no idea what I do in my business or my community, yet he is willing to conduct his own personal research and provide the driving community his diagnosis. The deeper I thought about this, the more I reflected on myself. I did this to myself for years. I judged what I was and who I was, based on the judgment of other people. Today, I won't stand being treated poorly or being ridiculed. For years, I allowed myself to be abused mentally. Here is what's even scarier — I see this self-deprivation in a lot of people I meet today. They are living below their potential as a result of false beliefs or misinterpreted information. What false beliefs do you have about yourself? What limiting ideas have you had about yourself that have proved to be untrue? How have false beliefs kept you from taking risks? How have you let false beliefs undervalue your true worth?

I have a friend I talk with from time to time, who is an incredible role model for me. Not because of what he has accomplished in his life, but because of his positive outlook. He is a constant source of encouragement to me in times of doubt. He is the one who encouraged me to take a closer look at my beliefs. One day when I was complaining about a particular business challenge, he asked me a series of questions. I began to answer in an automatic and negative sort of sequence. Halfway through the process, he gave up and told me that he couldn't help me with my problem. Feeling indignant at what appeared to be an apathetic attitude coming from a friend I trusted to give me encouragement, I asked, "Why?" He simply said to me, "I can't convince you that your venture will work because you've already convinced yourself it won't." I sat there stunned for a minute and then asked, "What should I do? "Would I be willing to have my convictions challenged?" he asked. I agreed, what choice did I have if I wanted his advice? What happened next was very interesting. He took me through each one of my objections and uncovered beliefs that I had about the way things seemed or ought to be. What we learned together was that I was holding onto ideas and thought patterns that were, not only stifling me creatively, but also breeding fear into all I was doing.

Once we completed work on my initial problem, I took the same principles and ideas and applied them into other areas of my life. I found I had been holding on to all kinds of false beliefs. It was like going back to my childhood, and for me, this process opened up creative ideas and possibilities I had let go of because of my linear adult thinking. I find it so enjoyable to watch children play today. They create and build with such abandon. They have no borders, no false beliefs. In fact, everything and anything is possible. When I think about the possibilities I have as a professional speaker or with the leadership of Mindware Design Communications, I need to think like a child and dream big. Otherwise, my adult thinking and false beliefs creep in and downgrade my entire plan.

In my study of the great thinkers and achievers of our time, I learned that they each rose above pessimistic thought patterns and created an environment that fostered and allowed the incubation of greatness.

By asking me questions, she had drawn out the reasons for my fear.   Why did I think I would fail? Why did I think the marketing plan wouldn't take? What did I personally lack in the process? I have talked about this in training sessions. Below, is a short list of beliefs others have talked about.

> I lack money.
> I'm too old/young.
> I'm too fat/thin.
> I lack talent.
> I lack confidence.
> I lack opportunity.
> There is too much competition.
> It has been done before.
> I'm not smart enough.
> I'm just not the kind of person who takes risks.
> I will fail.
> I don't have enough time.
> I need to plan more.
> I need to research more.
> I'll start tomorrow, this fall, next year.
> I don't deserve success.
> I've never done this before.
> I'm too shy.
> Success only happens to other people.

The list continues endlessly. These remarks came from people who had worked though and identified their key passions. They were put through a series of goal- setting and life-evaluating exercises and were faced with the fact that what they were currently doing, was not aligned with their true dreams. Once face to face with key issues, out came the false beliefs. They seemed to serve some kind of subliminal defense against change, to somehow insulate against their fears. Believing in a lie was easier than facing the fear associated with change. It's the old story of the devil we know is better than the devil we don't know. I can surely attest to this theory. I have spent more time worrying about things that could or might or should happen, only to reach the end of a journey and find all my fears were unsubstantiated. There is nothing in this world to fear.

Franklin D. Roosevelt said in his first inaugural address, *"The only thing we have to fear is fear itself."* All else is only circumstantial evidence that we tend to mount in the case against us. Be open-minded and willing to look honestly at your excuses, and you may discover more about your potential than you ever dreamed.

Sometimes perspective is everything when evaluating our fears. I like to define fear as *having a real present danger or an imaginary danger.* Let me explain with a story.

A few years ago, my wife and I decided to try something different. We enrolled in a character-building exercise, which required us to take a four-hour lesson learning three simple commands. The commands were: Get Ready, Climb Out and Go! Any guesses what we were learning to do? If you guessed skydiving, you are correct. During our four-hour training session, we practiced using an old metal frame of an airplane on the ground. The instructor had us run through the motions countless times just to make sure we had the process memorized before our jump. As we loaded up the small airplane, I began to feel ill. Practicing on the ground was one thing, but the reality of taking off in this tiny airplane was entirely different. They sat me at the front of the airplane, as I would be the first to jump. We sped down the bumpy dirt covered runway and soon we were off the ground, barely clearing the cornfield. At least that's how I remember it. We circled one thousand feet, we circled two thousand feet, and then we hit three thousand feet. Three thousand feet was the altitude we were to jump from. Once we reached three thousand, the side door of the airplane was opened. The wind rushed in and filled the little plane. It was surreal. As I looked only inches to my right, there was a straight drop of three thousand feet to the valley floor below. I began to think I was nuts for doing this. My lunch was in my throat and I was genuinely afraid for my life. After all, if things went wrong, they would go **very** wrong.

At this point, the jumpmaster slapped my helmet and yelled "Get Ready." This was the command to grab both left and right door jams of the exit on the airplane. The jumpmaster yelled the next command, which was "Climb Out." For me, this was probably the hardest command to execute. On this command, I had to physically climb out of the airplane onto the tiny little tire, while holding onto the wing's support strut. Keep in mind, this airplane still is flying at 80 kilometers per hour and it is very windy. It would be almost as windy climbing out of your car while racing down the freeway with only one difference — I was three thousand feet above the ground. The next command was, "GO!" This command was yelled at me after I had shimmied my hands up the wing strut and had removed my feet from the tire, leaving my body flapping in the wind. I was hanging in the wind like some want to-be-daredevil. The jumpmaster slapped my helmet and yelled, "GO!" I smiled and nodded with enthusiasm, but didn't dare let go. Moments later the jumpmaster slapped my helmet and yelled, "GO!" I smiled again and nodded but wasn't quite ready. Finally, on the third command with knuckles turning white, I let go and began my short free fall in both sheer terror and pure delight. Once I left the airplane and my parachute opened, the fall back to solid ground was serene and peaceful.

On the way down, I got to thinking about real fear and imagined fear. On this particular day, I had a healthy fear of heights and of leaving the plane without my parachute opening and this fear had a substantial consequence. I later thought of the many times I have been controlled by fear on issues that were not life threatening. Fears like presenting to a large group, investing money or taking a business risk.

This one experience helped me to put into perspective many issues, and now I make decisions, knowing that even if the worst happens, it's really *not* going to be as bad as bouncing in a cornfield. Sometimes, perspective is everything. Incidentally, my wife did not jump that day. We returned the following week when she completed her jump and was given an award. Jennifer got the Mile-High Gravol Award. She was the second person in the school's history to vomit into her parachute. I guess we all manage fear in different ways. (*Incidentally, Jennifer read through this manuscript before printing and approved this story. What a good sport!*)

Honest Feedback

One of the ways I have found to keep honest and free from outside negative forces, is by getting feedback from people I love and trust. When I question the way I'm thinking, I will ask a trusted friend for advice and see if my current assessment of the situation is accurate. This sounds like a simple task, but there are a few things critical to making this idea work. I surround myself with people I believe in and who know and believe in me. I was told early in my career that my "Circle of Influence" should be comprised of

individuals who hold the kinds of values and characters to
which I aspire. I was told to shed negative influences, to rid
my self of toxic relationships and people who are energy
drains. People who complain a lot and constantly seek out
conflict in this world…I leave these people behind.

When I look back at my life, I can see where I did well and
where I did poorly. I also can clearly see positive or negative,
in direct correlation with the company I kept and the fruit I
reaped. Today, I surround myself with winners. People who
are busy creating good — people who have an interest in
building, developing, and creating positive change in their lives
around them. Whether in business or in my community, I
want to be inspired daily. If I associate with the kind of
people who have a hard time getting up for work in the
morning or envisioning something better, it's only a matter of
time before I find my own energy and morale beginning to
slip. I choose my company very carefully today as I need
people more than I need any other resource on earth. It is
through people I am taught, inspired, encouraged and loved.
Without good people in my life, I am left with a desire to
succeed, but little direction on how to do it. This is one of
the reasons I read biographies of individuals who have done
something amazing with their lives. Their experience helps
me on my journey.

What I learned about the power of my "Circle of Influence"
was that I could employ the success of many to achieve my
dreams and goals. I also learned that I could help others
within my circles that are facing similar challenges and
obstacles. By plugging into a group of friends, associates and
mentors, you can grow much more quickly. I have a kind of
synergy with these people today and we can share ideas freely,
without the worry of criticism or ridicule. It's a safe place

amongst friends, to grow and learn. People helping others learn, grow and believe in their own possibilities and potential.

I remember one story that was told as a demonstration on how important other people are in our own personal journeys. The story begins with a man getting stuck in an emotional rut at work. As days turn to months and months to years, the man found that the rut had turned into a hole. The hole began to get deeper and deeper as time passed. The man wasn't a particularly bad guy. He was well liked, and had friends and a family that loved him. By all accounts, he was a normal person. What was different about this man was his circumstance in life. He made a few poor choices early in his career that led to the hole that now was his life.

This began to affect all areas of his life. He was suffering from financial problems, family problems, health issues, emotional dilemmas and a spiritual disconnection. For months, his family tried to fish him out of the hole. They tried ropes and ladders; they tried just about everything to pull the guy out and nothing worked. He continued to live in the hole, digging himself deeper and deeper as each day passed. After the family had exhausted their resources. They decided to try a number of different ideas to try and pull the guy out of his hole. They tried using a fireman, a doctor, and a pastor; finally, they brought a psychiatrist to the side of the hole to talk to the man. The psychiatrist asked the man what was going on and the man replied, saying he had made a few mistakes along the way and the rut he was in turned to a small hole, and then grew larger and larger each day until he was in a very big hole. The psychiatrist asked how he felt about the situation and the man replied, saying he was lonely, tired and afraid. All he wanted was to get out and go on with his life. He explained that for a long time, he felt helpless and hopeless with every day that passed. He could only see that he was digging himself deeper and deeper in this hole of despair. He also admitted that if something didn't change soon, he was going to lose all hope of ever getting out.

After several hours of talking, the psychiatrist came to his own conclusion and it wasn't good. He held a meeting with everyone who cared for the man in the hole and told them it didn't look good and that everyone should prepare for the worst. It was around this time a man from the back of the group raised his hand and asked if he could give it one last try. Friends and family began to inquire as to this man's qualifications and credentials. They learned he didn't hold a degree; he wasn't a doctor or a social worker. He had no serious involvement with religion or the health profession. It finally came down to one question. They asked the well-meaning man why he thought he could help the man in the hole. He told them at one time he was in a similar hole going through a similar experience, and that maybe with his past experience he could help the guy. He spoke with compassion and empathy because he had been in this situation before.

After a short discussion, the group decided it couldn't hurt to have him try. The man's name was Allan; the man in the hole was Bert. Allan prepared to do something no one in the group had yet considered. If he was going to be of service to Bert, he needed to meet him where he was, instead of trying to get him to come out of his hole. Without thinking about it, Allan jumped down into the hole and found himself face to face with Bert. The people on the surface were shocked and confused. They wondered how Allan could possibly help Bert by jumping down the hole to be with him.

From Allan's new vantage point, he could see how confused Bert really was. He was dirty and beat up. His fingernails where broken from his many attempts to dig his way out. He was shaking and shivering from the cold and damp conditions. Allan could see Bert was afraid, he could sense his hopelessness and desperation. His face was puzzled with frustration, fear and despair. He looked at Allan with tears welling up in his eyes and said to him, "Now that you're down in the hole with me, we're both stuck. We have no chance to get out, we're going to perish and be stuck here forever." This is when something truly special happened. Allan held Bert's shoulders tightly with both hands and with a firm look into his watery eyes and said, "There was a time I was stuck in this very hole. I know how real your feelings of hopelessness and despair are, because I personally have walked this journey. Here's the good news, Bert. Because I've been here before and survived, I know the way out. Follow me and everything will be all right."

A few hours later, both men climbed out of the hole of self-imprisonment. Allan's experience saved Bert. His ability to connect and understand his pain was Allan's secret advantage. Years later, Bert told his friends that Allan had given him specific instructions that day. He told Bert he would not accept any gift or accolade, the only way he could repay him was to look for opportunities to help others out of the same hole. He said you must "pay it forward" in order to keep the cycle moving.

All of us have experiences like this. We experience adversity in life and we grow through the process of change. The previous metaphor teaches me that the experiences that shape us as people can be used to help others. We all experience very different things in life. These collective experiences, when shared in a group dynamic or in a mentorship type of relationship, give us the ability to grow and learn from another person's experience. This concept is the basis for most of the world's self help and group therapy movement. Those individuals who have experienced and triumphed over a certain problem or addiction are given a set of tools to help others of the same circumstance. The relationship is based on the theme of identification and common circumstance. One person with a problem solved can help another person solve their problem by sharing their experience, strength and hope.

It may be true that not everyone needs to attend a 12-step meeting to get answers in life, but I am certain we all need people we can trust to help guide and lead us to the places we need to go. We often need others to keep our ideas about ourselves healthy and positive…to help encourage us and give us energy when we really need it…to help us believe in our abilities, hopes and dreams. I firmly believe in the counsel of many.

Rooting for the Underdog

Why do people like to root for the underdog? Why is it that when we see someone who is not recognized in an industry make it, we celebrate with just that much more emotion? Why do we cheer for the less favored to succeed?   I have a theory. I believe deep down, we all have at one time felt like the underdog. Let's face it, not many of us have won an Olympic medal, shot the winning goal for the Stanley Cup or achieved number one in a national sales contest. Most of us don't achieve first place; sadly, the majority don't even try. I have competed a great deal in my life, and have won my share. But this doesn't change the fact, in a different arena and a different sport, I still feel like the underdog. When starting something new or taking a risk, I almost always feel like the underdog.

The greatest underdog story I know is that of David and Goliath. David was the weakling of his brothers. He was not a warrior but a shepherd. When he heard of the challenge Goliath gave to the Israelites, he became disgusted and insulted to the point he wanted to fight. He approached King Saul and asked if he could accept the challenge on behalf of Israel. Saul told him he was only a boy and that he would surely fail. David tried to convince Saul by telling him he had many times been called to protect his flock against both the lion and the bear. Surely these challenges had prepared him for battling and winning against Goliath.

What was David's strength? What did he believe in beyond everything else? Why did David believe he would not fail? If we look at David's example, along with Reg's example, we see a few similarities. We see what looks like obstacles being turned in strengths. We see faith exercised in David's case. In the face of tremendous danger, David held steadfast to his belief and abilities and his faith in God.

Stories of faith and triumph inspire me. Mostly because they are more common than we think. They happen all the time and they happen to people like you and me. I can read, listen or experience ideas like these and work them into my own hopes, goals and aspirations. I can see myself succeeding because another "underdog" has made it.

I read a book by Og Mandino in my early sales career called, "The Greatest Salesman In the World." It is one of my favorite books and I highly recommend it to anyone involved in the world of selling. It is an inspiring story with action steps throughout the book. The one action step that I began using was self-talk and morning affirmations. The book encouraged me to read aloud several paragraphs that were designed to summon positive energy, and get you prepared for a positive and productive day.

This chapter was about believing in yourself and following your dreams. With that in mind, I have included an affirmation, which is fitting for this theme:

Recite this to yourself each morning:

Today is the day I will honor my dreams.
Today I will move one day closer to living and achieving everything I want out of life.
If today I am not feeling positive, I will remember that:
Somebody needs me today,
Somebody is thinking about me today,
The world needs my gifts and contributions today,
People are waiting to celebrate my successes today,
Someone admires my strengths today,
The world wants me to be happy today,
People love and depend on me today.
Today, I'm going to tackle the world with the energy of two people. I will not and cannot fail.
Today I will succeed.
No matter what happens, I am set on making today count!

So far, on my journey, I have discovered that life is like a parade. Either you're in the parade or you're a spectator, left standing in the street once the last clown has passed. I'd rather be in the parade than standing in the street looking for some clown.

7 Questions:

1. Do you truly understand your personal value and potential?

2. What emotional "Radio Station" are you tuned to?

3. Have you honestly analyzed your personal belief system?

4. What tools do you use to motivate and inspire yourself?

5. Do you have a positive Circle of Influence in your life?

6. Do you have a mentor?

7. Starting today, what will you change to move closer to your definition of success?

3

"I don't believe in letting the future take care of itself. Planning does not give you full control, what it does is give you direction and purpose."

Dr. Alan Haynes

SECRET *3*

Building *your* Life Manifesto

E very great leader has a plan. Planning is the foundation upon which great nations, great companies and great people build. When you think of it, nothing ever really happens without first a plan or a vision. Can you imagine next year's new cars being developed without an engineering plan, or flying the nation's airlines without some kind of flight plans? What would happen if your business had no projections or your child's teacher had no curriculum? These examples may sound exaggerated, but when you think about it, we live in a world that puts more importance on planning the wedding than preparing for the marriage. More of our time is spent getting set for a vacation than preparing for a career. Why is it that we expose our lives to this randomness? Why do we set ourselves up for failure, wishing life would provide all we need, without any effort on our part?

There are several reasons, but most often the case is simple. People put off plans for their lives and themselves simply because it interferes with a busy schedule. After all, when is there time to plan a career? We are just too busy working! When life is busy, it's hard to have long-term vision. How am I supposed to think about five years from now when I'm barely making it to Friday? My point is that this kind of thinking can kill your dreams. Each one of us has unlimited potential for success. We all have what we need to find and fulfill our dreams. This is a fact. It's true.

So why don't more people self-actualize and fulfill their life's dreams? It could be because they never start moving in the right direction. We often think, ponder, and dream about how life could be, or should be or maybe one day will be, but we never make the first move. Without a starting line, there is no finish line. If the starter pistol fails to sound, there is no race. My point is simple. Without written, definable, quantifiable goals, your hopes and dreams likely will not come to fruition. This is fact number two. If you can't show me your plan on paper, your chances to succeed in business, finances or even weight loss, are greatly diminished.

I met a friend of mine the other day that was going through a really tough time in his career. I asked him what his plan was and in less than 10 minutes he told me about six different directions he could take. I asked him a simple basic question, "If I were to blindfold you and spin you in a circle for five minutes and then ask you to use a rifle and hit the center of a target five-hundred-yards away, could you do it?" "Of course not," was his answer. Why? Because, he said, " I would be disoriented and dizzy from being spun and I'm wearing this blindfold." "Precisely!" He looked puzzled. Then I asked him the following questions:

How can you hit a target when you don't know which way to aim?

How can you hit a target you cannot see?

How can you hit a target you do not have?

We talked further and he started to define his goals, building a plan and steps he would need to take in order to accomplish them. My enthusiasm on this topic of goal setting and planning is the result of first-hand experience. I remember hearing about a university study on a graduating class in the late 50s. The class was polled and it was discovered that only three percent had written definable, quantifiable goals.

When they revisited this same group 20 years later, they found some amazing results. The three percent who had written goals had achieved more. They were happy and fulfilled and they had acquired more wealth than the entire remaining 97 percent combined! The power of goals gave them a road to follow and their life's dreams came true.

I heard this story in the early years of my recovery. I thought to myself, "What would it hurt if I tried the same method?" Immediately, I started to delve deep into my heart and soul to find what I really wanted to accomplish in life. I wrote it down. I recorded what contributions I wanted to make to the world. When I was done, I had a binder full of lists and goals. Accomplishments for my life and career.

But let me take you back even further. I remember the day like it was yesterday. I was sitting with my drinking buddy on a Friday night. I was in my early 20s and I told my friend what I was going to do with the rest of my life. I was going to go back to school, and I was going to help kids. I talked about future wealth and business success. I went on and on for a long time and when I was done, I had planned out my future. The interesting thing was later that week, I actually wrote it down on a piece of paper and then completely forgot about it. My life would need major alterations if these goals were to be met. None of this made any sense until later on in my life when something miraculous happened.

I had totally forgotten about that list until a few years later when I went through the same exercise sober. I was committed and spent several hours processing and producing a plan. When I was done, I had a set of goals for my life. I wrote them down.

Years passed and it was nearing the end of the 90s, when rummaging through some old boxes I found the original list. It was written on an old piece of cardboard. The writing was scribbled and hard to read, but it all flooded back to me. As I read, my jaw dropped. I could remember writing these years before. I obviously had not put any faith into the process and had stuffed it into that old box. I was curious as to how these "original" goals compared with my more recent goals. I went to my binder and compared the two lists. It was amazing — they were almost identical. There were very few differences. The original list had a few more action steps written down, detailing how I was going to escape my lifestyle at that time. You see folks, I had begun the process of believing I could transition my lifestyle and had written it down some two years before it actually began to happen.

As I went through both lists, I started to check off item after item I had already completed. Toward the end, I was stunned. What I had envisioned the first time and had written the first time had such a powerful impact on my subconscious, that years later I was still on track for achievement. I can't begin to make sense of why or how this works. I'm a simple person in many ways and the explanation behind this kind of phenomenon range from the deeply spiritual to the science of the inner mind.

However, this is what I do know — IT WORKS!

I don't understand the engineering fundamentals behind electricity, but I do know that when I come to work and turn on the lights and computer, they work. I don't understand why my car runs (neither does my mechanic and I have the bills to prove it), but I do know that when I turn the key, the engine starts.

Here's my point — you don't have to understand the reason why, if you know the reason how. A good friend said to me that often times I will try to intellectualize a problem when I don't need to. Somewhat offended, I asked him what he meant. He explained that if my house was on fire I'm the kind of guy who would sit in the fire and wonder how it got started. A normal person would simply look for an escape. Life's dreams and achievements start with a written plan. How all this works with our subconscious and the universe will remain a mystery to me. All I need to know is that it does work.

If something as simple as setting goals can help a hopeless case like me, just imagine what it can do for you. What are your dreams? Write them down — now! How do you begin your list? What steps do you take? How do you even know what you want to do for the next 30 years? Discovering what is most important for us requires a little deep thinking. Building a "Life Manifesto" can take several months or even years to develop and refine. The most important thing is to begin. I have several exercises that I invite you to do. First, you need to understand what is really important to you. You need to get deep into your values and core beliefs. A simple way to define what is most important in your life is to answer the following question:

If my life were to end in six months, I would want to...

I want you to take some time now to start thinking and writing down what comes to mind with this question. Don't spend any time evaluating your thoughts; just write what comes to mind. You can always come back later to further define these thoughts. What is important is that you start meditating and processing free thought. This kind of thinking is not something we do every day so it is important to write down everything. It's brainstorming for life. By placing an emphasis on six months to live, we force ourselves to think within a time limit. After all, life does have a time line. This exercise helps us focus and prioritize our most important goals.

By asking yourself what you would like to do if you had only six months to live, you begin to see what your core values are. The question regarding the time limit will help you clearly define what is most important in your life. All too often, we get busy doing urgent tasks and ignore our most important work. We run around always meaning to get back to our true passions, but day-to-day living constantly interrupts us. As you think about what goals are most important, prioritize and think about what absolutely must get done before your life ends in six months.

Something very interesting happened on Sept. 11th, 2001. We gained perspective as a nation. At 8:30 a.m. that morning, the people in the office towers of New York City's World Trade Center had high priorities. Business meetings, clients to call, presentations to prepare...then tragedy hit. We all will remember where we were when we heard the news. The horror of that day will stay with us forever. That was the day our priorities changed.

If you could choose and know when you will die, if you truly did know six months from now that your life was going to end, what would you need to accomplish to give your life meaning? I've interviewed a number of elderly people as a volunteer. And what I find interesting about many of the individuals that I've known, is the ones who fulfilled their life dreams had no regrets and therefore did not fear death. However, the ones that greatly feared death were those individuals who looked back on life and had regrets about things they had never attempted. I believe it was hockey legend, Wayne Gretzky who said, *"You miss 100 percent of the shots you never take."*

One day at a bus station, I spoke with an older gentleman and he shared this with me, *"The tragedy of life is not that it ends so soon, but that we wait too long to begin it."*

Is your list completed? OK! Now make another list with new criteria. Imagine what you could do if you had absolutely no limits, on time and money. Answer the following statement:

If I won the lottery tomorrow and had all the time in the world, I would...

The reason we use the metaphor of winning the lottery is that for a great number of people the greatest "perceived" obstacle is money. I talk to a lot of people and they always say, " I don't have time to start a new business; I'm too busy just trying to make ends meet," or "I just don't have time to lose 20 pounds." Imagine you did have the time to follow your dreams. Often, we dismiss ideas that are very attainable because we simply don't have the money. We don't think creatively about ways to raise capital or how to bring in a partner. Most times we simply dismiss great opportunities in life, because we lack the creative thinking needed to raise the cash. Think about visionaries who have established a clear picture of what goals they wanted to accomplish, whether it was building one of America's largest corporations or going back to school. They focused clearly on their goals and managed to find the people and resources necessary to finish their journey. History is glorified with inspirational stories of entrepreneurs and pioneers who set reason and obstacles aside to pursue and conquer their dreams.

While you're doing this exercise, I want you to pretend you're Thurston Howell III from Gilligan's Island and you have all the money in the world and that financial resources are not an issue for you. Or maybe you're the distant brother-in-law to Bill Gates. I also want you to think that you have all the time in the world. Forget about the kids for a moment, forget your family commitments, and forget business pressures and that busy career. Think outside the box, and believe you have no limitations whatsoever; picture what your deepest desires might be.

When you complete this exercise, you will have a draft of the most important things that go into your Life Manifesto. It may seem silly or even awkward to think in these terms, but I know it truly does release the powers within the conscious mind and unlocks deep and important passions. It shows us the things we could do if we have the opportunity. What's interesting is that everything you have on your list today can be accomplished. You do not need to win the lottery; you do not need to give up all of your commitments. Starting tomorrow, just one day at a time, one week at a time, and one month at a time, you will start to move toward what is most important in your heart, your mind and your soul. You can truly begin to accomplish what's most important for you.

When I started my life over in 1991, I had to make a list of goals. I had to think beyond my immediate situation. If you told me in 1991 that I was going to become the CEO of a multimedia corporation, make my first million before I was 35 and become a professional speaker, addressing corporate audiences worldwide, I would have said you were out of your mind. At that time, I had **very limited vision**. If I've been guilty of one thing in my life, it would be not reaching beyond my immediate grasp.

Over the years, I've had the opportunity to have great men and women mentor me in business, personal and spiritual matters. They always told me I had great potential, especially early in my career. In the beginning, many people believed in me before I believed in myself. Isn't it interesting how other people can see our great potential, yet we have a hard time seeing it ourselves? I have a friend who's a tremendous artist, extremely gifted and talented beyond words. His artwork inspires me, yet every time I compliment him he responds by saying, "It's nothing." If only he could see his true talent, if only he could see how far his gift could take him, if only he had vision.

Remember the story of the blind teacher and the crippled student. For many years, the two worked lovingly together. The crippled student would describe in great detail all that he saw and experienced with his sight. On their many field trips together, the teacher would act as the boy's legs and the boy would become the teacher's sight. One day at the beach, a man was watching the two as they compensated for each other's weakness. The crippled student described the ocean waves and the beautiful coastline that stretched for miles. As the boy sat in his chair, he described to his blind teacher the elaborate colors of the sunset, the seagulls as they soared in the wind. He described the orange glow and the foam of each crashing wave. What a man watching from afar saw next was heart-warming, for the blind teacher reached down and grabbed his crippled student and placed him on his shoulder and said to the boy, "With your sight I can see, with my height you can see further, please tell me what you see." The teacher learned to have vision through another. He became the student by using the resources he had available. Often times in life I too feel blind, not knowing which way to turn, or which way to go. I need somebody to describe for me what they can see and what possibilities may lay ahead.

By creating a Life Manifesto you have a clear direction.

Imagine the car is packed and you're ready to go, your first ever cross-country trip. From the White Mountains of New Hampshire to the rolling hills of San Francisco, you're going to see it all. You put the car in gear and off you go. First stop, the Baseball Hall of Fame in Cooperstown, New York. A little while into the trip you need to check the map, because you've reached an intersection you're not familiar with. You panic for a moment because you realize you've forgotten your map. But you say, the heck with it because you know where you're going. You take a right, change the radio station and keep on going. Unfortunately, you never reach your destination; you're going the wrong way.

Too many of us treat goal setting the same way. We dream about where we want to go, but we don't have a map to get there. What is a map? It's a directional path that we choose, and with discipline, we follow. What is the difference between a dream and a goal? The written word. But we need to do more then simply scribble down some ideas on a piece of paper. Our goals need to be complete and focused, much like a road map, and that is the purpose behind the rest of this chapter. If you follow the seven stages to creating a Life Manifesto as outlined below, you will be well on your way to becoming an expert in building the road maps to your future success.

"I don't believe in letting the future take care of itself. Planning does not give you full control, what it does is give you direction and purpose."
Dr. Alan Haynes

Here's a system I've learned and refined over the last 12 years. Nothing in this system is particularly new or original; it's the same basic truths that have worked for many people throughout the ages. These are my seven stages to creating a Life Manifesto.

The Seven Stages to Creating Your Life Manifesto are:

1. Write it

2. Categorize it

3. Define it

4. Measure it

5. Have a timeline

6. Be positive and use present tense

7. Review it regularly

Stage Number One: Goals must be Written

The difference between a dream and a goal is the written

word. For any goal to be effective, it needs to be written. Writing helps us define exactly what it is we want, where we are going, and why it is we want it. The fundamental idea behind a goal is to have something we can refer back to as we journey to succeed. A busy life with career, family and community commitments, can stint all good intentions. But with a written set of goals, we have a map to come back to as we move toward our goals — this makes us accountable to ourselves. We can reflect daily, weekly, monthly and annually on how well we are doing, and what changes we need to make to stay on target. These written goals are the tracks that hold the train on course.

The train has all the power to move quickly and swiftly down the track, but if one of the tracks is not aligned, we all know what will happen.   Our lives are a lot like the train — immense energy, tremendous power, but without focus, this energy and power is out of control, going nowhere. There are two choices — you can choose to plan a life for yourself or you can choose to take whatever life is handed out today. For years, I lived a default lifestyle. I did nothing and accepted whatever came along.

Today I recognize, **we don't get what we deserve in life, rather we get what we negotiate for ourselves.** A lot of people I meet are living life that way. By failing to plan, they plan to fail. I'm not suggesting that every individual who doesn't have a Life Manifesto is going to miss out on some of the great things in life. What I am saying is that those who set a life plan and have a clear definition of who they are and what they want, will find more successes.   Remember the three percent?

Imagine, if you will for a moment, how the great leaders in the business world got to where they are today. Did the president of General Motors simply wake up one morning and decide he was going to be the president of General Motors today? No, what the president of General Motors likely did was set out very early in his career what he wanted to accomplish as he climbed the corporate ladder. Great musicians, artists, literary talents throughout the world did not simply wake up one day to find themselves successful and at the top of their field. They worked long and hard, days, weeks, and hours, committed to what they saw as their life goal.

Great accomplishment does not come in the mail.

Great accomplishment comes from dedication, perseverance, sheer determination and focus on a goal. Did you know that only five percent of the world's population has a written, clearly defined, plan for their life?

Stage Number Two: Goals must be categorized

In order to have a balanced Life Manifesto, goals must be created in several categories. Think for a moment about the different roles you play in life. We all belong to a family and have some kind of home life. We all have some form of career, we all belong to a community and let us not forget issues of spirituality and health. For myself, I've broken my Life Manifesto into many different areas. First, the kind of man I want to be, as a husband, a father, a businessperson, and as a member of society. I want integrity and character. I want to be positive, responsible, caring and loving. For me, it's important to address issues of attitude in order to grow into the man I want to be.

There also are important issues for me to consider regarding my family, the kind of husband I want to be, the kind of father I want to be to my little girl, and the kind of son I want to be to my mother. Family goals are as important as career goals. All too often, we read about the successful entrepreneur or executive who now is going through his third divorce.

Last weekend, I had the pleasure of meeting Mr. Wayne Cotton, who taught me an important issue around planning goals in 90-day cycles. He suggested structuring a 90-day calendar and to define personal time first. Then to focus three other areas of time management. Take your calendar and schedule all personal time for family, rest and relaxation. This focus is on the most important things in your life — *you* and *your family*. The next is career. Based on where you want to be in 5, 10, 15, 20 years from now, what will you need to accomplish in the next 90 days or in the next year? What kind of accreditation or senior executive positions would I like to hold in my company? What one or two things would I like to have accomplished in my business life that would say to me, I've truly arrived?

Move onto the area of financial and material goals. I think all of us have a vision of what that dream car looks like or what our dream home might be. Some of us fantasize about that special kind of boat we'd like to own or maybe you'd like a motorcycle. Focus also on the financial well being of your business and personal life. The kind of security, stocks, bonds, and investments you may want. The financial situation you would like to be in, one year, five years and 25 years from now. By focusing on these goals today, you can draw into the present moment and the next 90 days what needs to be done in order to hit these financial and material goals.

Driving the car of your dreams doesn't happen in a week or two, unless of course you win the lottery. It takes a long time of planning and cultivating a series of small attainable goals to finally get to the place where we can realize all the things we dream of.

Now we come to issues of spirituality and faith. As a Christian man, I want to invite God into all areas of my life. When my life gets busy, this becomes increasingly difficult. I need to set aside time each day to connect with God by reading my Bible, attending church service and socializing with other men and women of faith. Some of the most successful people I know in the business world start each day with prayer. By committing themselves to prayer and meditation and connection with a higher power, they are able to go out into the world each day and practice integrity, character and honesty. Having had a deep spiritual event occur in my life reminds me to always "stop and smell the roses" and always give thanks for the blessings in my life.

Another very important area we must consider is that of our physical well being and personal health. At the age of 36 years old, I went into the hospital the day after Christmas with a stomachache. Seven weeks and four major, life-threatening surgeries later, I was released from the hospital with an abdominal scar from the top of my chest to below my belt. I spent the following year recuperating and fighting for my life. The doctor told me the reason I was in such an ill state was because of my personal neglect, no exercise combined with a stressful career. He told me if I wanted to live beyond 40, I had better start to exercise regularly and begin healthy eating. Remembering those long painful nights in my hospital bed keeps me committed to a daily exercise regime. I also try to eat a healthy, balanced diet.

One of the last areas that I look at is the area of community. It's extremely important that we give time, money and talent to our community. We build great communities by volunteerism. Each of us has a cause or special place in the community where we like to invest time and money. I work a lot with troubled youth in the area of drug prevention education. I also have a soft spot for the homeless and hungry. Whatever your cause or passion, commit yourself and set goals around it.

I remember the story of a boy named William who was raised in Nottingham England in the late 1820s. In his neighborhood, there was a man named Mr. Crookshank. He was a vagrant with an alcohol problem, but a lovable man just the same. William used to have long conversations with Mr. Crookshank and began to truly care for and love this old man who was always down on his luck. One evening, a gang of local thugs took to beating Mr. Crookshank so severely it left him brain damaged. When young William asked his mother where Mr. Crookshank was, his mother lied and told him Mr. Crookshank had moved away. Truth was he had died. William made a bold statement to his mother that day when he declared that, *"When I grow up, I'm going to help people like Mr. Crookshank."* That boy grew up to become Sir William Booth, founder of the Salvation Army. By committing himself to his community, he founded what is now the largest charity organization in the world, dedicated to helping all people, including those like Mr. Crookshank. Because of William Booth, I had a warm place to sleep and a hot bowl of soup when I needed it most. You may never know how your gift of time and talent may truly affect someone's life.

There may be other areas where you want to focus that I have not covered. Maybe there are places you want to go, relationships you want to rekindle, relatives or friends you wish to reconnect with. You may want to explore educational accomplishments or even artistic endeavors. The above is simply a template to help you start writing your Life Manifesto today.

Stage Number Three: Goals must be Defined

One of the worst things you can do when writing a goal is to create a goal that is not definable. You need to be as specific as possible. In fact, the next three secrets are about the definition of your goal. If it's a new Jaguar that you want, what color is it? What year is it? How much will you spend on it? When will you acquire it? How do you imagine it will feel sitting behind the wheel and driving it?

The only way to get a clear picture of what your goals look like is to have clarity of vision by fine tuning and clearly defining what your goals look like when they've been acquired or accomplished.

Stage Number Four: Goals must be Measurable
Like in Stage Number Three, your goals need to be measurable. Having non-measurable goals opens the door to too much variance. Always remember that you can change your goals anytime, but it is important from the beginning to make sure that they are clearly defined and clearly measurable. If my goal was to lose 25 pounds, it might read something like this:

On Nov. 15th 2003, I will weigh 25 pounds less than I do today. I plan to lose these 25 pounds in increments of five pounds per week starting Jan. 7th. I will do this by reducing my caloric intake by 500 calories per day and by walking on the treadmill at the gym for 40 minutes, three times per week. When I reach my new weight, I will enjoy fitting into clothes I haven't worn in over a year.

The above is a great example of the definable and measurable goal. By placing measurement on a specific goal, we can monitor our daily, weekly   and monthly progress. This makes it easier to change or alter plans in order to reach our goal. It also gives us important feedback to keep our motivation high on days when things seem too difficult.

Stage Number Five: Goals must have a Timeline

Very important in setting goals is the creation of a timeline. Very large goals need to have benchmarks. Creating a goal to have the number one multimedia company in Vancouver is a great goal and by building in stages, I will further define this goal and give a measurable, definable timeline to this task. One of the short-term goals might be to grow sales revenue by 40 percent in the next year. This goal helps me bring into focus a timeline that will allow me to weekly monitor our progress and success.   It also will allow me to take a series of these smaller goals and build a modular plan to succeed at the larger goal. My large life goals have been defined with a timeline to be accomplished by a certain age. Prior to writing this chapter, I studied my own Life Manifesto and was surprised to see that a number of goals I wanted to have accomplished before I was 40 had already been met.   Next to writing your goals down, having a timeline is probably the most important.

When considering timelines and how they work in your Life Manifesto, you will need to consider how you are going to segment the short-, mid- and long-term goals. Short-term goals are the things that can be done in the next few weeks and include things to do today like vacuum the house, make 10 phone calls, mail out six packages and go to the bank. Mid term goals are those goals we want to accomplish within 90 days to six months. Long-term goals usually are goals we want to accomplish within 10 to 25 years or in a lifetime.

I also have a list of what I call, "BHAGs." BHAG stands for "Big Hairy Aggressive Goals." My Big Hairy Aggressive Goals are the really big things I want to accomplish in life. Issues relating to finance, family, community and health. One of the BHAGs that I have is to run a marathon and climb Mount Kilimanjaro before I'm 50. By having goals listed in different timelines, we can bring into the present a goal that seems so distant and ominous. We can do something today that will work toward accomplishing a goal that may be 15 years out.

From my friend Dr. Alan Haynes, I learned to tackle the biggest jobs each day. He taught me that one of the ways to move toward our biggest goals is to do five extra new things every day. These five new smaller goals each day are our little goals that will help us conquer our greater goals. On my desk in the office, I keep old business cards that have blank backings (recycling is good). Each morning, I take one of these old business cards, flip over on the back, and write down five new things I'm going to accomplish that day. These are not on my regular " to do" list but rather, over and above what I'd already planned.

By completing five new tasks per day, I complete 35 new tasks per week, 150 new tasks per month, and over 1,800 tasks in one short year. The power of doing a little over a long time can help us tackle our BHAGs. Try this for one year and see how much you accomplish!

Stage Number Six: Goals must be Positive and Written in Present Tense

Another thing to do is to write your goals in the present tense. For example, if you want to own a new Harley-Davidson Sportster motorcycle in the year 2005, write it like this: *Today's date is Jan. 15th, 2005 and I am the owner of a brand new Harley-Davidson Sportster motorcycle.* Now you might be thinking this is insane, but it's the exact kind of thinking that pollinates our subconscious mind and begins us moving toward the goal. By writing the goal as if it's already happened, you trick your subconscious mind because it does not know the difference. Therefore, you create a mental environment that helps you attract and gravitate toward   those things that you want to accomplish. Again, I don't know why this works but I do know that it does.

One other issue to consider when writing goals — write them in a positive sense.   If one of my goals were to invest only with professional help, I would not write: *I won't be so stupid as to do my own investing in the future.* I might write: *In the future, I will be confident in my investing strategies by always consulting a professional financial advisor.*

Stage Number Seven: It is important to Review Regularly

Once you create your Life Manifesto and you have it in a binder beside your desk or on your bookshelf, you need to review it regularly.   A goal, written and unattended, will die. I review my 90-day goals sheet daily.   I review my annual, five-year and 25-year plan monthly.   By constantly focusing and reviewing where I want to go, I can bring into the present tasks I can complete to help move me toward my mid- and long-term goals.

I also hold myself accountable to personal, spiritual and company goals.   I do this through an accountability group I have with a number of men I respect. We meet on a regular basis and share what we want to accomplish over a certain period of time. We each complete our individual worksheets, and then we re-convene a month or two later to review how we each did.

It is important when picking people for your Circle of Influence, people with whom you will share your goals that you choose those who are positive, with vision and energy, which will support your endeavors. I highly recommend that you do not share your Life Manifesto with individuals who may discourage, belittle or ridicule your ambitions. They are all around you, the soothsayers of doom. I have five or six people in my life that I hold in high esteem. These are the people with whom I share my deepest desires, dreams and goals. However, there are a number of people around me with limited vision; I would selectively share only portions of my vision with them.

In addition to having an accountability group, I also have mentors. Again, like members of an accountability group, mentors need to be people you look up to, you trust, and you believe will help you move toward your goals. Mentors are people who guide you in life. They share wisdom and counsel to champion you along the way. I have had the luxury of being mentored by some really great people. It's because of these mentors that today *I am a mentor*. When I needed wisdom and counsel, these people were at my side to guide, teach and advise me on all matters important in my life. This book and my life is testimony to setting goals for personal achievement, sharing these goals with friends and helping people daily move toward their own personal fulfillment and joy.

Now that you have learned some of the fundamentals, think about the individuals in your life who can help you achieve these goals. Bring these people into your Circle of Influence. Take the biggest goals you have and the biggest dreams you have and reach for them..

Jim Pattison once said, *"Individuals that have the ability to think big dreams have the ability to achieve those big dreams."*

I believe it, because today I'm living my big dreams.

7 Questions:

1. Do you have a set of life goals that you're following today?

2. Have you reviewed your Life Manifesto recently?

3. Do you have a 90-day plan for success?

4. Can you name five things you could start today that would contribute to your Life Manifesto?

5. What 25 things could you do in the next week to contribute to your dreams or desires?

6. What's stopping you from writing out your goals?

7. It all begins with a plan; will you begin *yours* or simply start reading the next chapter?

4

No discipline seems pleasant at the time, but painful.
Later on, however, it produces a harvest of righteousness and peace
For those who have been trained by it. Hebrews 12:11

SECRET *4*

Your Declaration *of* Independence

In the last chapter, we talked about the importance of creating a Life Manifesto. Having goals and a plan for your life. This is only the beginning of what I call the **Trinity of Success**. The Trinity of Success involves three very distinctive areas. First, it involves setting the goals. Second, it involves committing to those goals, and third, it involves taking action on these goals — which we will discuss in greater detail in the next chapter.

In this chapter, we are going to focus on committing to these goals. I met a man at a convention in Oklahoma City one year after the federal building disaster. He was a simple, yet deep man. He had an aura about him that radiated peace and integrity. As I got to know this man, I learned that after the bombing took place, he left his work to be of service during the days, weeks and months that followed that tragic event. He explained to me that when he began to volunteer his time, it was only a temporary commitment, but as need and demand grew, he was faced with a decision not a lot of us could make. He decided to leave his well paying career and give all his time and effort to caring for the victims of Oklahoma City. As I listened to this man, I was fascinated by his resolve and his commitment to carrying through with his decision. His story is not one of those typical "everything turned out OK" kind of stories. In fact, things did not turn out well for my friend. By taking time off, his career was jeopardized. He missed promotions and potential future positions within his firm. He began to suffer financially and eventually he had to move into a smaller house and drastically reduce his lifestyle, all for the sake of his burning desire to be of service.

As I got to know my new friend, I could tell this man was definitely committed, in fact with some of the things he told me, I thought he should be *"committed."* It all became crystal clear when I asked him one question, "Why had he continued to stay committed when things got bad?" He told me when he began his work, he was simply doing what thousands of people in Oklahoma were doing. He showed up to help out his brothers and sisters in need. Like many, he wanted to do his part, both physically and spiritually, to support the people in his community. As his involvement became deeper, he felt a need to commit whole-heartedly to this project until all needs were met. He made a decision early on that no matter what happened, he was going to see it through because in his heart, he was committed.

He looked at me and said this, **"Commitment is the willingness to carry through with a decision long after the mood in which it was created is gone."** By defining what he needed to do, he continued to hold himself responsible for his goals and commitments, even during times of duress and

turmoil. This friend taught me something valuable about myself that day. He shed some light on why, for so many years, I had not met with success. It wasn't that I did not want to succeed, it was **that I never followed through!**
He explained that on the toughest days, he reminded himself that these people needed him and that his commitment to see this project through was a personal choice he had to deliver on. I kept in touch after our talk that day and something wonderful happened in his life. He eventually lost all interest in his previous career and realized that the only reason he had pursued it in the beginning was money.

By committing to this new goal and taking direction from his heart, he ended up going through this metamorphosis and reinventing himself. He had found a new career. His opportunities began to materialize when others witnessed how he gave 110 percent and was so dedicated. Today, he tells me that the journey was long and hard, but if he had to do it over again, he would do so in a minute.

In the one line he taught me, in order to have my dreams come true or to experience any kind of peace with myself, I have to commit to my goals. Commitment is easy when you're all fired up for change and you're excited about the goals you've just written. You're at your kid's school, you volunteer and then forget only to be reminded when the phone rings two weeks later. Or you begin your exercise program on January 1st, telling yourself this year is going to be different, only to relapse into old habits after the second week. We all do it! So how do you keep your motor running? How do you keep the fires burning?

Commitment is hardest when things don't go as planned.
You're deep into your journey and you're faced with the toxic
idea that you want to quit. This is far harder than expected.
Don't do it! Don't quit before your miracle happens.

Many times in my life I have quit just short of victory. I may
have been afraid or discouraged. I may have been just lazy and
had no focus on what was most important. Either way, today I
know how important it is to gain resolve and vigilance when
addressing my Life Manifesto and passions.

Let me share with you one of the most inspiring stories I
know about commitment. It begins with a question: When
did the United States of America receive independence from
England? Most people respond to this question with the
answer, July 4[th,] 1776. But that's not entirely true. You see
what July 4th, 1776 represents is the day that independence was
declared!!

Here's why I find this story so fascinating. The story of the
birth of America completely embodies the Trinity of Success.
In the beginning, the forefathers of America sat down and
WROTE out their ideal way of living. They documented
precisely how they want to live and for what they stood. This
is now one of history's greatest documents. The forefathers
then took this detailed set of goals or America's Manifesto, if
you will, and began committing to the fight to have it become
a reality.

On July 4th, 1776, the last signature was signed, and the
Declaration of Independence was presented to the King of
England. As a result, the newly established America
continued the fight to free itself from England. This is what
we today know as the War of Independence.

Why am I using this as an example of commitment? Simple — if you were one of the 56 men who signed that document on July 4th, 1776, you had to be committed. There were no half measures. You were either in or you were out. There was no turning back. There was a war to face with the end being either a new America or a renewed state of control by England.

Imagine for a moment the level of commitment it must have took for some of those men to sign their names. I would have been terrified. Imagine what might have happened if England had won the war. For treason against the king, those men would have hung by their necks. Was it a risk? Yes, it was! Was it assured victory? No, nothing ever is. Was it worth committing to? Absolutely!

The forefathers of the United States believed in their dream of a free nation. They believed it was worth the commitment, regardless of the potential outcome. When I think about leaders of this caliber, I am inspired. After all, the goals I commit to likely will never have the consequence of death attached to them. My risk might be my pride, my time or my money. Not my freedom or my life.

If America did not achieve independence on July 4th, 1776, when did they achieve it? It actually came some seven years later on Sept. 3rd, 1783. It was then that the Paris Peace Accord was signed between England and America and the Revolutionary War officially was over. They declared Independence (America's Manifesto), then committed to their goal and spent the next seven years fighting to make it a reality.

Today, I think about what I have learned on my journey. I am reminded of the many times I have had to simply commit to my sobriety. That some days this was the only thing I was able to focus on. On bad days I need to remember, I am committed to staying clean and sober. No matter what, getting loaded simply isn't an option. Slowly, day after day, year after year, I have watched my life rise up from the ashes of a broken and ruined existence. How did I do it? Simple — one day at a time.

Funny thing about this life we live, we are able to plan the future, compose complex thoughts, while contemplating dreams and visions. But the reality is we only get one day at a time to make them come true. Life is given to us moment by moment. This is either good or bad, depending on the headspace you're in. On days when life is troubling, I want nothing more than to close my eyes and be in next week or next month. The only difficultly with this fantasy is I would never get to truly grow and learn, if I was not tried by fire, so to speak. Many of my greatest lessons have come from my greatest mistakes. What has helped me the most is knowing what I stand for. What my purpose and vision is. And what I am doing today that lines up with my manifesto.

Recently, I had the pleasure of attending an event held by The Canadian Red Cross. Former New York City Mayor Rudolph Giuliani was the speaker. He spoke about what happened to him personally when the events of 9-11 unfolded. He immediately studied great leaders of the past and analyzed what they had done in crisis. The one constant he found in his research was that great leaders who had lead people though hard times had one thing in common. They all had conviction. They knew what they stood for and what they were committed to. Once he understood this concept, he applied it to his own circumstance. He became a true leader in a time of confusion.

In his speech, Mayor Giuliani said something like, "You cannot lead until you know what you personally stand for and believe. Once you know what you stand for and believe, it is easy to get people to follow your direction because your every action is driven from that core."

I really appreciated his take on the subject, as he would know best what it takes to lead under pressure. In his time after the events of 9-11, Rudolph Giuliani was effective because he was committed to his belief. He had a clear vision of what needed to be done and made his decisions based on principles, beliefs and his commitment to leadership.

The idea of knowing what you stand for is probably one of the most liberating and energizing feelings. The concept of commitment to one's beliefs or goals is refreshing because it eliminates so many other choices. Think about this for a minute. The obvious benefit of goal setting and commitment is that it gives us direction and purpose. A map to follow. A course to take. What's not so obvious is that it eliminates so many other choices that can, if not guarded, rob us of valuable time and energy. Today as a committed father and husband, I do not entertain the idea of adultery. Why? Not because I no am longer attracted by the opposite sex, but because I made a commitment. I took a vow. I have family and parental goals. I have a set of values I live by and they don't include any negotiation on this matter.

The same holds true in business endeavors. Many of my friends over the years have jumped from one opportunity to another, never really pursuing or committing to one idea. One of my old mentors and friend taught me early that I needed to protect my resume so that it didn't look like a road map when I was 45. He told me that the sooner I committed and stayed in one place long enough, good things would begin to happen. He told me overnight success usually takes 10 years. Today, I recognize that success in business often comes from perseverance more than timing. It's easier to succeed in life over time instead of trying to be clever by finding the newest and most recent venture to exploit. I applied this idea and have no regrets. Friends still approach me and ask if I'd like to invest or jump on board different businesses and opportunities. I simply reply, "I can't as I am already committed to other ventures that consume all my time and resources."

Knowing what you don't want is as important as knowing what you do want. Your foundation is where you lead from and on which you must base all actions.

Commitment to Service – Rigo's story

Some organizations are built on commitment to customer service. I so enjoy this kind of commitment when I find it. As a business owner, I like to study and learn from other companies finding unique ways to bring value to the market place. Service Master is a great example of this on a large scale. Other not-so-large companies build great little businesses by committing to two simple things — the best service and value available. I had experiences like this in two completely different restaurants. One in Canada and one in Mexico. My first experience was in Mexico at a little palapa restaurant, just outside of San Jose Del Cabo at the tip of the California Baja. During our vacation some years back, I was given, as part of the condo rental, an older model Parisian Station wagon to drive during our two-week stay. This wagon was longer and more awkward than anything I had ever driven, as I was accustomed to driving smaller vehicles. We left for the evening to visit a restaurant everybody raved about. We had heard the food was great and the service was excellent. We quickly located the restaurant, with its little wood-painted sign, "Rigo's Restaurant." The dirt road that led up a small hill revealed to us that because Rigo's was such a great little place, the parking area was full. We had two choices. We could head out to the busy freeway and look for another place to eat or we could try and find a place for me to park this rather large vehicle and enjoy some famous food. Because the road lead up a hill and back out to the freeway, I decided I would try something different. I looked into my mirror and saw that there may be just enough space for me to back my vehicle down the hill and off to the right side, leaving room for others to pull in, giving me a parking space.

I backed my car up, but to my horror, the hill had a very steep drop off, and before I could react, I was axel deep in sand, mud and dirt. My wife and I looked at each other. There we sat in our shorts, sandals and newly purchased Hawaiian T-shirts looking like a couple of dumb gringos. As I began to panic, some of the local folks pitched in to help us out of this not-so-nice predicament. After 45 minutes, two trucks and five men helping, we managed to lift the vehicle out of the rut and safely to the top of the hill, where there was now an open parking spot.

I was impressed. When my wife, Jennifer, and I entered the restaurant, we found that one of the men who had just worked in the dirt to get us out was the owner himself, Rigo. He disappeared for 10 minutes and when he came back, he had on fresh clothes and it appeared he had taken a quick shower. As he came to our table, I thanked him and tried to give him some money for his trouble but he would not accept it. Later when the restaurant had slowed down, I asked Rigo why he had helped me. He told me this, his business was about providing happy vacation memories and that anything he could do to help his customers achieve this, he was more than happy to do. I asked him if that included digging customer's cars out of the dirt. He winked at me and said, "I'll bet you'll never forget your visit to Rigo's Restaurant."

Rigo was committed to a set of principles that I'm sure were tied to the goals of his business. He knew what his role was and when the time came, he delivered. He recognized this was service. Although not food service, it was very much a part of his personal commitment to his customers.

Every time I'm in San Jose, I visit my friend, Rigo. We eat from the expensive side of the menu and tip obnoxiously high, all because of the service we received on our first visit.

The second example of commitment to customer service is a famous restaurant in Vancouver called The Cannery. Jennifer and I had heard about the great seafood and wonderful service so often, we felt it was our civic duty to try the place out. We waited until we had a special occasion and that date finally arrived. Several days prior, I called to make reservations. I asked to be seated at 7 pm for a sunset dinner. The woman on the phone was ever so polite as she asked if this was a special occasion. I told her in fact it was our second wedding anniversary. She said 7 pm would be fine.

When the day arrived for our special night out, I had several business challenges and I had to try to make time that evening. I called the restaurant and asked if we could move the reservation up to a new time of 5 pm. Once again, the woman answering the phone was ever so gracious and replied, "No problem, Mr. Roberts." I thought this was going to be the last shift in my plans, but yet another emergency required my time and I needed to shift dinner to 6 pm. I am very lucky that I have an understanding wife; I wasn't sure the restaurant was going to give me the same latitude. Once again, I called to move my reservation and yet again received a "no problem" at the other end.

The business day finally ended and Jennifer and I were on our way to celebrate and enjoy our long-anticipated evening out. If you have never been to The Cannery and you plan to visit Vancouver, I recommend it highly. This Vancouver gem is located on the shipping docks, just east of the city. Although it is in an industrial area, the service and food truly is world class. When Jennifer and I arrived, we were greeted warmly and escorted to our seat, which was one of the finest in the house. It was on the second level with a view of the harbor, Stanley Park, The Lions Gate Bridge, and all the spectacular North Shore Mountains. Because this was late August and we had arrived at 6 pm, we were in for a treat as we dined and watched the sun set on this beautiful city of ours.

As we sat down, our server, Jorge, greeted us. With his impeccable manners and refined social graces, I knew that we were in a very special place. Now I travel a lot and have dined in some pretty fancy places, but this was different. When Jorge handed us the menu, I was delightfully surprised to see, *"The Cannery is pleased to celebrate Joe and Jennifer Roberts' second wedding anniversary."* As I looked at my wife, I saw she was moved. How touching that this restaurant would think enough of us as customers to commit to this simple, yet powerful way of recognizing our special day. This was marketing genius at work. I also thought to myself, we'd be coming here often. The evening was splendid; the food was the finest and the view spectacular. As my wife and I held hands, we enjoyed the golden sunset sky in our newly discovered "favorite" restaurant. Jorge was perfect in his every action and the experience was an "11" out of 10.

Why is it that examples of this exemplary service stand out so boldly? I think it's because not many people or businesses take the time to commit to quality and service. The reason we recognize it is because of all the extras, out of the ordinary that make it extraordinary! Because they commit to a higher standard, people notice the little extra care and attention. The interesting thing about both examples is that this kind of distinctiveness usually costs nothing. It often only takes one creative idea to stand out.

Recently, my wife and I bought our first home. We were waiting to buy our dream home and had held off, but the declining interest rates became so attractive, we simply couldn't wait any longer. The house we were renting in Burnaby was listed for sale, so we began our search for a new place a little further out in the City of Coquitlam. After an exhaustive search, we found exactly what we wanted. Interestingly enough, we had a clearly defined set of criteria. We knew what amenities we wanted, what kind of neighborhood and school as well as a defined price range. On Oct. 1st, 2002, we moved out of our old place but before we moved, we began getting direct mail from moving companies. They sent us letters that read something like, "We heard you're moving and want to introduce ourselves to you in case you need a good reliable moving company." I thought this was a cleaver idea but was quickly discouraged to see that they all did the same thing.

Within a week, I had received four or five offers that all read the same. I thought to myself, this type of promotion could be much more effective if they simply twisted it a bit and truly catered to the stress and challenges of moving day. A serious commitment to customer service might include actually lending a hand to the outside issues that face us when we move. From providing a blank moving checklist to helping us organize all the tasks from hooking up hydro and changing the mail address to enrolling our child in school. Or locating the local recreation centers and churches in our new neighborhood. Or what about a simple blank spreadsheet for expenses and budgeting? Goodness knows there always are large, unexpected bills that come up when moving. A checklist with the company name on it would go far. I also thought that a moving company might be smart to build an alliance with a child nursery or pet care business or a pizza company to help with the stress that occurs on moving day.

Here's a promotion that did come in my mailbox that I thought was brilliant. Home Depot sent me a personalized letter that said, "The Home Depot wants to welcome you to the neighborhood. Improve your move with this $10.00 Gift Card."

The Home Depot sent ME $10.00. WOW! What an idea. No strings, no coupons, no special offers, just ten bucks cash. Here's a company that likely has committed millions of dollars to this program just in Canada — forget about the costs if this is running in the United States. If five percent of North Americans move each year, the Home Depot may be giving away a truckload of money. Sound crazy? How can they do this and expect to turn a profit? Easy. What are they banking on? Why is this not a risk? The Home Depot is counting on the fact that guys like me will receive this gift and with gratitude return to the Home Depot again and again, hence building customer loyalty and a long-term relationship that will be highly beneficial to the long-term strategy of their business. It may take The Home Depot two or three visits out of me before this market expense is justified, but I'm sure they have done the math. By understanding customer behaviors and committing to a long-term relationship with homeowners, they are investing in future sales. Smart!

Now what about commitment to quality and excellence? I recently gave a keynote speech and as an example, I used French sculptor, Fredric Auguste Bartholdi. He was commissioned to design a sculpture that now is one of America's finest symbols of freedom. Fredric was given the task of building The Statue of Liberty. Why am I talking about this particular example of commitment to quality and excellence? Well, in my studies I learned something very interesting about Fredric's level of commitment. It turns out that all the copper sculpting was done by hand. Everything we see was done by hand, dismantled in France into 350 pieces and shipped to the U.S. to be reassembled on the awaiting pedestal the Americans had built.

What I found interesting is that in spite of the quickly approaching timelines and increased cost, Fredric insisted he continue to provide the finest of craftsmanship. He spent countless hours refining and perfecting his masterpiece. Today, the statue stands on Bedloe's Island over 300 feet above New York's famous harbor. At the time of construction, this massive copper and steel monument was one of the largest of its kind. Toward the completion, Fredric insisted the head of the statue be finely detailed. He spent several extra months and thousands of dollars hand sculpting the braids and hair behind the great statue's crown. Why is this so special? Because this extra time and huge expense came from pride and commitment to quality and excellence. You see, in 1875 when this work was begun, there were no buildings remotely close to this statue. No one could see to appreciate the thousands of additional hours spent refining the braids and hair. Airplanes had not yet been invented. There were no helicopter tours, or commercial planes flying overhead to appreciate his work. When Fredric decided to spend the extra time, he did it out of pride and a spirit of quality workmanship. Impressive indeed.

I've talked a bit about businesses and their commitments, but where I've learned the most about commitment, is from my friends and heroes. One such friend is a guy named Jimmy D. Jimmy, like me, didn't come from a life of privilege. In fact, he came from a harsh place. As a child, his family life was dysfunctional and he was a victim of neglect and ill parenting. At an early age, Jimmy found himself in trouble with the law and by the time he was an adult, he had "earned" himself a long stay in Joyceville Penitentiary in eastern Ontario. In prison, Jimmy was taught how to hate. He was taught that all other emotions are useless and that hate, and only hate, would keep him alive while he spent his time inside.

Years passed and eventually, Jimmy left penitentiary life. He found himself spiraling out of control as a reckless drug addict. One day, he decided things had to change. He entered a detox facility to try and get sober. He, like many others, found himself at the end of his journey, having to choose between continued drug use with promises of only prison or death, or face the fear and uncertainty of change and recovery from addiction.

He chose recovery and began his long journey home. I met Jimmy when I first got sober in Belleville, Ontario. What I found amazing about him was even with everything he had been through, and with all the odds against him, he was managing not to just survive, but to do really well. Jimmy was less fortunate than most of us; he had very little education growing up. He could barely read, but was a proud man that wanted to contribute in the meetings like everyone else. That is why he insisted on always doing some form of reading. Those of us around Jimmy were patient. Over the years, Jimmy's reading skills improved. At the start, it would take him five long minutes as he read a short paragraph out loud. Every now and then, someone from outside our community would attend the meetings and would try to help Jimmy pronounce the words. They would only make that mistake once as Jimmy would give them a glare and snap at them, "I can manage just fine, thank you very much." He was still an angry man and we wanted to respect his dignity and help foster an environment that would help him grow, learn and feel accepted. That's why we never interrupted him. We let him sound his words out until he could read them with confidence.

As Jimmy's confidence grew, so did his love of helping others like himself. He committed to this new life of his and began to take part in the service of others. We lived in this little town and about 20 kilometers away, was another even smaller town. A support meeting in that town had just been started by one of Jimmy's friends, one that would help other recovering people. It was now his turn to give back. He dedicated himself in mid summer but the response was slow. By November, things were not much better. Jimmy would make his way over the 20 kilometers sometimes driven by friends, but most times by hitchhiking or walking. He never stopped trying. Every now and then, one person would show up and Jimmy would share his story and experience with them. Through that entire winter I watched, as every Thursday night, Jimmy would head out to the highway in the dark and blistering cold to travel to this meeting where most times no one showed up. A few times, I thought he was crazy for staying so committed until I asked him why he did it, even though the response was poor. He told me that his gratitude needed to be expressed in the physical sense. That he could not simply say he was glad that life was better for him. He had to act. He also told me that where he came from, your "word" was everything. If you gave your word or committed to something, you had to follow through.

Many things have changed for Jimmy over the years. The little meeting that no one showed up to ended up growing and flourishing, touching the lives and families of hundreds of people. Jimmy grew too. In the mid 1990s, Jimmy reached a milestone in his life. After many long, hard months of study and hard work, Jimmy, all decked out in his Sunday best, took stage at our local college and received his high school diploma. If you know Jimmy, you know him for his smile and the sparkle in his eyes. His shining spirit helped him stay committed through the long hard years it took him to change and reintegrate into his community. Jimmy is one of my heroes — a guy who taught me that nothing was impossible if you had friends, courage and the sprit to continue in the face of adversity.

Whether you are building a business or planning your family's future, you need the special energy that comes from having made up your mind. It refreshes your energy and gives the whole project direction and purpose. Along my road, I have had many good friends like Jimmy to teach me lessons about life. Some have been teachers; others have simply been in my view lens while they were living their lives.

One dear friend of mine is Ian Selbie. Ian is the President of Power Marketing, a sales effectiveness company. He also is the author of, *"If you were arrested for selling would there be enough evidence to convict you?"* Ian has mentored Mindware's sales team and me for a number of years. In fact, I credit a large part of Mindware's success to the sales strategy and tools I have learned from Ian.

In his book, Ian quotes an idea that he learned from Robert Schuller at a seminar held in Vancouver in 1994. I really like the wisdom of Schuller's approach. His take on issues of positive attitude and human spirit stand the test of time.

Here's what he taught: Successful people all have a plan, which comes down to these four things:

> Start to *Play*
> Stop to *Pray*
> Prepare to *Pay*
> Plan to *Stay*

Start to Play is what we discussed in Chapter Three about building your Life Manifesto. Delving deep and getting to the root of what your true passions are. What really turns you up and on? For me it is leadership and selling but most of all, professional speaking, because of the difference I can make. I love sharing life with people. I still am bewildered today when people tell me my story has helped them through some really tough stuff. I can't express in words the feeling I get after a successful event, hearing the client tell me my services helped make their event successful and helped their people solve problems.

For me, playing is about doing things I love to do. I spend the odd Saturday in my home office planning, preparing and stargazing personal and business objectives. Jennifer will ask me why I'm working on the weekend and I try to explain that this isn't work, it's play. This is what I do in between work.

Schuller then talked about stopping to pray. As a Christian, I want to invite God into my life each day. Recently, my spiritual mentor had me commit to an exercise called seven minutes with God. It's a simple, yet effective way to align myself with my faith and higher power each morning. It includes a short time to pray for guidance, the reading of a chapter or series of Psalms and a four-pronged prayer approach, which includes adoration, confession, thanksgiving and supplication. This whole exercise takes seven minutes. I can do this quite easily. I also have found that since I have committed myself each day to a spiritual time to read, pray and listen, life takes on a deeper form and fulfillment. When I stray, I always pay. I pay with disjointed mental thinking. My mind becomes noisy and cluttered. Whatever your faith or belief system, I encourage prayer, mediation or quiet time each day to connect spiritually and mentally. It's a tough world out there and you don't have to go it alone!

Point number three made by Schuller was prepare to pay. Nothing worth going after in this world is free. Some things are no-fee but not free. Building a successful career means you will need to invest time, energy and resources. The same holds true for a successful marriage and family life. Expecting a thing to simply work out in the long run is wishful thinking and if that's your strategy for success, good luck! Paying the price for achievement, sobriety or wealth takes time and perseverance. I remember a famous movie star responding to the comment that he had become an overnight success. He responded somewhat indignantly when he explained that he had been dedicated and working hard since he was a teenager and that his "overnight success" was in fact the culmination of over a dozen years of grueling effort, never losing sight of his commitment to one day "be a star." One time at a golf tournament, a famous golf pro hit a hole-in-one. During the interview the reporter said, "You must be real lucky to have hit the hole-in-one." The golf pro responded by saying, "I know this may sound funny but I was aiming for the hole, why would that make me lucky?"

The price you pay is your "admission" to a better life. Lanny Flores, my first sales coach and mentor, taught me that the harder you work, the luckier you get. I had an audience member at one of my events tell me afterward how she thought I was so lucky, that success, wealth and happiness had come my way. I thanked her but later on the plane ride home, I started to resent the comments as I thought about all the effort and hard work I had put in to get to where I am today. Yes, I have been fortunate where others have not. But the reasons why have to do with hard work, effort, commitment, and paying the price for success. Lucky? No, I didn't win the lottery; I worked hard toward my goal.

One of my favorite bible passages is this: "No discipline seems pleasant at the time, but painful, later on; however, it produces a harvest of righteousness and peace for those who have been trained by it." Hebrews 12:11. Zig Ziglar said it well when he said, "You don't pay the price for successful living, rather you enjoy the price." What you pay the price for is bad living and poor decisions. Today I understand that short-term gains often equal long-term pain.

Lastly, Schuller talked about planning to stay. Some of the biggest decisions I have made involved huge, scary risks. But I was in it for the long haul. I enjoy jumping in today. I was on the sidelines half my life, watching the lives of other people roll by. Inside, I was too afraid to start because I thought I would fail.

Today, I know there are no such thing as losers — just those who are not yet winners. No matter how long it takes to conquer or succeed at something, I'm willing to stick it out and see what happens. If nothing else, I will learn from my mistakes. During an interview, Thomas Edison was asked what he would be doing if he had not invented the light bulb. He said to the reporter, "I certainly wouldn't be chatting with you, I would be still be trying." Edison said that he didn't feel he had failed, rather he had learned hundreds of ways it would not work.

We are here for a lot longer than we think. Whoever said life is short was old. Life is long and beautiful, with time to fulfill our every dream and aspiration. There was the story of the 60-year-old man who, after a visit to his doctor, was told he was going to die within a year because he was lazy, ate wrong and had a miserable outlook on life. He finally decided to give up the high cost for low living and created change in his life. He immediately changed his attitude, his diet and became physically active. Today, he is 77 years old and just finished running his ninth Hawaiian Marathon. Who said life was short? There's always time to turn things around. Look at Jimmy D. or Reg or me… all of us and thousands more with similar stories are living our dreams today because *we can*. And so can you!

Your life's dreams will not fulfill themselves. Not committing to something will produce varied results, most often discontent. Here's the good news though. You always have free will and choice. It is OK to change your mind or direction if, after a fair period of evaluation and analysis, you feel it's time for a change. But first, give it all you have. Commit with abandonment and expect victory. Start today by determining how you want to live. Decide what you no longer will tolerate in your life and build your personal Declaration of Independence. Your only task after that will be the battle for its future reality and that, my friend, is what life's really all about.

7 Questions

1. What are you willing to fight for to become your reality?

2. What price are you willing to pay?

3. What will you commit to today?

4. What is the worst consequence if you fail?

5. How could your job or business profit from your commitment?

6. If you change absolutely nothing, what will life be like five years from now?

7. What hopes and dreams have you not committed to, but will now?

"Go confidently in the direction of your dreams. Live the life you have imagined"
Henry David Thoreau

"You can't build a reputation on what you are going to do."
Henry Ford

SECRET 5

On *your* Mark, Get Set, Grow

E ven with a set of goals and a firm commitment, you are not likely to find success without action. This is the third element in the Trinity of Success. Take action! Thus far, we have talked about setting your goals and committing to those goals. Now comes the time when rubber meets the road. Today is the day I must make it count!

Have you ever bought a lottery ticket and stuffed it in your wallet, stuck it on the your cork board above your desk or on your refrigerator? What happens every time you walk past that ticket? Are you like me; you glance at the ticket and wonder if it's a winner? Oh, if only it be true, your financial troubles would be over forever. Then life and reality creep back into your consciousness and you continue with your busy day with a vow to validate that ticket at the very next opportunity.

I do this. I'm sure everyone has. What's interesting is that your chance of succeeding and winning the lottery usually are really slim odds. I once read that you have a better chance at getting struck by lightning twice in the same day as you do winning the lottery. So as a responsible adult, I made other retirement plans. I also made other plans for success that give me the control. What's interesting about the lottery ticket is that I'm sure many **real winners** have walked past their winning tickets many times before they finally checked them, only to discover their great fortune. Imagine being a millionaire and procrastinating three weeks to find out. What if your ticket was a winner today? What if all you had to do was cash in and accept your prize?

This is what I am advocating throughout Chapters Three, Four and Five with The Trinity of Success. That quality life you want. That dream marriage and family you desire. The big house and nice car. They're all waiting for you to be redeemed. There's only one catch. You have to do the work to get there. Sorry, there's no lottery office to drive to and accept your winnings. The winnings are in your Declaration; your level of commitment determines your winnings. You determine what you want. When you think about it that way, it's even better. I get to choose exactly what I want in life, I can sculpt and create a life I imagine, not just collect a pile of cash. I truly can have it all.

There are similarities between the lottery and a successful life, however. Some of your friends may envy you. There will be those out there that will want to take it from you and it takes work to hold onto your success. But in the end, it's worth every minute of it.

Acting on your Freedom

On Sept. 22nd, 1862, the Emancipation Proclamation was issued by Abraham Lincoln, which stated that on Jan. 1st, 1863, every slave in American was to be free. Two years later, a man was in a southern state and witnessed a group of Black workers toiling in the fields. As an abolitionist, he wanted to know if this group of workers were acting slaves or hired help. When he approached the workers and asked, they told him they were in fact slaves. He asked if they had heard about the Emancipation Proclamation placed into law over two years prior. They replied and said they were told it didn't apply to them. Their "owner" had lied to them and said that this Proclamation was meant for other slaves, not them.

The man was stunned to think that these people who were freed over two years prior had continued to live in bondage. He began to explain the details in the simplest way he could think of to them. Telling these good people that they no longer needed to subject themselves under this kind of oppression. That they were free to leave and start a new life. Once this news traveled throughout the their community, most of the workers abandoned their post and left to start a new life.

Sadly though, months after the abolitionist's visit, there still were a small few that refused to believe or simply could not manage the issue of change and continued living their lives in chains.

What's this story have to do with the Trinity of Success? Everything! Especially if you consider the idea of action. If you believe that for whatever reason you cannot succeed, you simply won't try. You may not live today in a world with physical oppression, but almost everyone I talk to has admitted they have had limited vision at one time or another. They believed false things about themselves and stopped trying or dreaming because they felt it was futile.

Here comes the good news. YOU ARE FREE! You do not need to live your life in mental bondage. You can start today by saying goodbye to limited thinking and negative beliefs. You no longer are governed by events of yesterday. Your future is spotless and **today is your day to act.**

What a liberating thought. I'm FREE! Free to choose, free to think, free to act, to dream, to give, and to love. I am free to live my life in this great land of ours, striving for what makes me happy. The prison walls have been torn down, nothing but blue skies ahead. I know it's going to be great, because I can see it clearly in my mind.

Say goodbye to those pesky demons and negative thoughts. You're going on a journey, never to return to this place again. You will change, grow, expand, and become the person you've always dreamed of being.

If you don't believe what I'm saying right now, then you are choosing to stay behind. And quite frankly, you may have valid reasons for doing so. Far be it for me to judge where you are today. I just want you to know that if you do not choose to exercise your freedom and liberty today, you can choose to do so at a later date. Because now you know the only one suppressing you is **YOU.** You always have held the key to set yourself free.

When I was young, my mother showed me how to do laundry. She taught me to always check every pocket before putting the clothes in the washer. She explained that this was to make sure you extracted all items before the wash cycle to avoid any possible messes. She explained that although I had gathered and placed these items in my pocket, by the time laundry day came, I would have forgotten I put them there.

Most folks I meet forgot what they put in their pockets. I thought about this later on as a leader. In essence what I do when I'm on stage speaking or working as a manger or leader, I don't give anything. I don't bring anything. All I do is get you to stick your hand in your pocket and tell me what the contents are. **YOU** have the answers. You hold the key to set your life free. I'm just telling you where to look for it. It's in your pocket right now. It's been there all along.

And we shall be then, henceforth, and forever free.

I worked briefly for a courier company as a territory manager after my stint with Minolta Canada. In retrospect, I thought it was going to be exciting, but it turned out to be a nightmare. Within my first week, I found myself having to justify my lunch break to my newly appointed boss. What I learned about this experience was I never want to work for someone else — ever again. As an experienced salesman and manager, I always had based my time schedule around my sales performance. If my sales numbers were good, it was nobody's business how I spent my time. At least that's what I thought. After all, I always have worked for straight commission, I don't believe in salaries or trading time for money. I believe in trading talent and performance for money.

Anyway, this new company did not agree with my take on time management and we were at our first impasse. I knew early on that my decision to join this new firm was a mistake. I felt sick, as I had spent a lot of time, energy and money, making this decision to leave one industry and join another. The thought of abandoning it now made me shudder. I did know one thing, however. If I was feeling this out of sorts this early in the game, something definitely was wrong. Could it be I made the wrong choice?

It just so happened that I joined the company around the time the national sales convention was being held. In less than two weeks after hiring me, they flew me to Toronto for training and to take part in the festivities, which for this company were grand. They spared no expense on the event; it lasted three long days, with the grand finale being a black tie event with a well-known professional speaker. At the event, I began to feel like I didn't fit in with this new crowd. I felt alienated and different from everyone. No one seemed to reach out or welcome me, which was fine. I guess they had their own pre-established social groups. But this further had me analyzing whether or not this was a company I wanted to invest my future in. I decided I would take the time in Toronto and make my decision before the flight home as to whether or not I would stay or go. I wanted to make a commitment on this issue either way. I could not afford to be wishy-washy. I needed to know if I was in or out.

On the third day of the convention, there was a speaker that really spoke to me. His name was Vince Poscente, and he was a former Olympian who competed as a Speed Skier in the 1992 Winter Games. Vince had us do an exercise that changed my career path. He got us to close our eyes and visualize what our perfect day looked like. He then had us do some work around our dreams, visions and hopes. He asked us similar questions that I asked in Chapter Three around what our passions were and our true dreams. He said to us, *"If you could do anything you wanted starting now, what would you do?"* It hit me so hard I opened my eyes. I found myself standing in the room with 600 other people, all of us under the direction and leadership of this one speaker. It was quiet and I could feel the energy from the speaker and the people. He was guiding, teaching, inspiring and helping us think differently. When my eyes opened, I heard myself say, **"I want to do what you're doing. I want to speak professionally and help people like you're doing right now."** He then told everyone to open their eyes and asked them this, "Why aren't you doing it? What's holding you back? What will it take to get you moving in the direction of your dreams?"

I was mesmerized by Vince's performance and now had clearly made up my mind as to what needed to happen. I would leave and pursue my path as a speaker. What I found ironic about this story is that the company that hired me had spent all this money on a great speaker, which, in the end, persuaded me to leave their company and follow a totally different path. I think in the end it was probably best for everyone.

The plane ride home was rather interesting. I was sitting in between the big boss for Western Canada and my local department manager. The big boss asked me what I thought of the convention. I told him it was fantastic. I learned so much about the company and myself and was excited about my future. So excited in fact that as soon as I got back to the office, I was tendering my resignation. Needless to say, he was a little taken back. Not quite the response he was looking for. The remaining four-hour fight was quiet.

If you ever read this Vince Poscente, thanks!!

What the point of this little rant is, that for a long time I had a winning lottery in my pocket. I had been walking around with all this potential prosperity but had failed to cash in on it for one silly reason or another. Imagine the power of having Bill Gates write you a check for whatever amount you desired and then taking that check, placing it in your pocket and forgetting or neglecting to cash it. How would you feel if when you reached the end of your life and you were shown what great riches you had but never cashed in on? All the missed experiences, neglected dreams and lost opportunities. I don't want that to happen to me.

I remember the story of the desert nomads who were given a vision one night. They were told that between now and the end of their journey that week, they would be both happy and sad. They then were given simple instructions to load their saddle packs with stones. Not completely understanding the message, many of them only put a few stones in their packs. They saw no value in transporting stones across their great journey. The voice behind the vision was accurate on both predictions. At the end of their long week, they arrived at their destination and unpacked their saddles. What they discovered was the stones had been turned into diamonds and precious jewels. They were happy that this had occurred, but sad that they had not packed more.

Life is like this parable. So much potential, yet we leave a lot behind.

I'm big on the importance of time because I lost 10 years of my life. I often ask myself, "What would life be like if I hadn't made all those poor choices? Where might I be today?" Not that I have regrets, it's just that life offers us so much and yet I see myself and others leaving so much on the table. I'm reminded of the line in an old rock-and-roll tune that said: "You fritter and waste the hours in an off-hand way, And then one day you find that 10 years have got behind you,

No one told you when to run, you missed the starting gun."
When I first got sober, I had to make many decisions. I had
no idea what I wanted to do with my life. All I knew was that
I didn't want to live as I had been living. I made one of the
best decisions I could have made by taking action and going
back to school. By going back to school, I began to stimulate
my learning skills. I began to learn the social skills I would
need in my personal and business life. Going back to college
really prepared me for the challenges and opportunities. I
would face. Here's what's funny. When I began college, I fully
had intended to go into social work of some kind. After all,
with my background, I would be a natural in that field. I had
a vision of why I wanted to go into the social work field, but I
didn't have a solid direction.

After a semester of General Arts courses, I discovered I
would really like to try and learn more about business and
commerce. Numbers always had fascinated me, and so had
dealing and interacting with people. Long story short, I
changed direction six months into my college career and today
hold two degrees in business.
My point is, when you're busy doing something related to your
Life Manifesto, opportunities will arise, new information will
become available, and you ultimately have the choice to
reevaluate and change your direction. What I did for too
many years is think about things, talk about things, but never
did anything.

Today, I understand the power of getting started. Kinetic
energy is the energy of motion. Any object that is moving has
kinetic energy. When we start moving toward something we
want, we initiate a life force that gives your project positive
kinetic energy.

Newton's Law of Motion

Newton's First Law of Motion: Every body continues in its state of rest or of uniform speed in a straight line unless it is compelled to change that state by a net force acting on it.
Newton's Second Law of Motion: The acceleration of an object is directly proportional to the net force acting on it and is inversely proportional to its mass. The direction of the acceleration is in the direction of the applied net force.
Newton's Third Law of Motion: Whenever one object exerts a force on a second object, the second object exerts an equal and opposite force on the first.

Take action – learn on the fly – don't wait for everything to be perfect before you move. Move now! Gone are the days when you had time and resources to: Get Ready, Aim and Fire. In today's fast-paced world, you had better learn to Get Ready, Fire and Aim. Remember — bullets are cheap.

I have moved forward on so many projects just because I had the courage to take a chance. Yes, it's true, you can get stung using this philosophy, but there are greater risks in sitting idle. There is a certain genius in beginning something, even if you don't have all your ducks lined up, so to speak. This drives analytical personalities crazy. People who pay great attention to detail find this doctrine uneasy and hard to follow. They are great at doing many detailed tasks but lack the necessary speed to move quickly. They tend to get caught in the analysis, to a point of paralysis. They produce much less than their counterparts, who are willing to move and risk.

On the other hand, work produced by the analytical personality always is top shelf material. Well researched, highly detailed, with no room for error. I think that's great but what if timing is everything? What if you need to see results fast or you want to save time and money by simply testing out a theory? That's when quick and dirty shortens the learning curve.

Lets face it — the concept of perfection in our imperfect world is ludicrous. We are delightfully flawed people (I'm so glad I'm not alone on this), and adherence to perfection is ridiculous. Did you know that baseball is one of the only games that recognize *errors* as part of the game? How do errors occur? Errors occur naturally in the course of play. Make a mistake and they write it down and charge you and your team with an error. Life is a lot like baseball. It's impossible for us not to play in the game. There are three inevitable stages. One, you're born; two, you die; and three, you fill the in-between time with something we call life. And what is life but time to fill? If we consider this, we have to look at what we want to do with this time. We also must give time the respect it's due. The neat thing about time is that it's indiscriminate. It doesn't matter who you are, how rich or important, you cannot negotiate time. Even the term, "Time Management" seems ridiculous. You don't manage time, you mange the events within time. So how important is time? What is its true value?

Imagine....

There is a bank that credits your account each morning with $86,400. It carries over no balance from day to day. Every evening, it deletes whatever part of the balance you failed to use during the day.

What would you do? Draw out ALL OF IT, of course!!!!

Each of us has such a bank. Its name is TIME. Every morning, it credits you with 86,400 seconds. Every night, it writes off, as lost, whatever of this you have failed to invest to good purpose. It carries over no balance. It allows no overdraft.

Each day, it opens a new account for you. Each night, it burns the remains of the day. If you fail to use the day's deposits, the loss is yours.

There is no going back. There is no drawing against the "tomorrow." You must live in the present on today's deposits.

Invest it so as to get from it the utmost in health, happiness and success! The clock is running. Make the most of today.

To realize the value of ONE YEAR, ask a student who failed a grade.

To realize the value of ONE MONTH, ask a mother who gave birth to a premature baby.

To realize the value of ONE WEEK, ask the editor of a weekly newspaper.

To realize the value of ONE HOUR, ask the lovers who are waiting to meet.

To realize the value of ONE MINUTE, ask a person who missed the train.

To realize the value of ONE-SECOND, ask a person who just avoided an accident.

To realize the value of ONE MILLISECOND, ask the person who won a Silver Medal in the Olympics.

Remember that time waits for no one. Napoleon Hill said it best when he said, *"On the chess board of life your only real enemy is time."*

We convince ourselves that life will be better after we get married, have a baby, then another, get a new job, get a new house. The truth is, there's no better time to begin living than right now! If not now, when? Your life always will be filled with challenges. It's best to admit this to yourself and decide to get busy anyway. So, treasure each day that you have. Don't let another day pass without taking action. And remember — time waits for no one!

So, stop waiting...

> ...until your home is paid off
> ...until you get a new car or a new job
> ...until you go back to school
> ...until you lose 10 pounds
> ...until you gain 10 pounds
> ...until you finish school
> ...until you get married
> ...until you get a divorce
> ...until you have kids
> ...until your kids leave the house
> ...until you retire
> ...until summer
> ...until fall
> ...until winter
> ...until spring
> ...until you die!

There is no better time than right now to take action. "Do not wait; the time will never be 'just right.' Start where you stand, and work with whatever tools you may have at your command; better tools will be found as you go along."

I want to make mistakes. I want to rack up error. I want to learn, grow and be all that I can be (without joining the army).

I don't want to wait another minute for it to begin. I must take action today, because today is all I have.

After college, two things happened to me. I found myself living in eastern Ontario surrounded by a great many friends, but without the economic environment needed for me to succeed. As a young man fresh out of school, I was under the misconception that the world, somehow, owed me a decent job and lifestyle. I was wrong. I went from being the honor role student and college star to the junior sales person without a parking spot. It was quite scary at first. I knew I had the talent, but wasn't sure if the little town where I lived was big enough to support my hopes and dreams.

After hanging around for 18 months, working in three different sales roles, I decided to take control of my life and make a really tough choice. I could continue living in this small town surrounded by people who loved me, and slowly watch my dreams fade, or could make a break and see what else the world had to offer.

I decided to move to BC as soon as I had enough money. Therein lies the catch. After graduating, I had never managed to prosper past one month's rent. I was living hand-to-mouth and financing a move out west was simply not viable. Refusing to not be discouraged, I started a financial feasibility study and determined that by using credit cards and borrowed money, I might just make it. With some creative accounting and determination, I arrived at my brother's place mid-May, 1996. The day I arrived, I was greeted with a Starbucks coffee. Being from the east, I had no idea what a "Starbucks" coffee was all about. Starbucks had not quite spread to Ontario. That night. I laid on my brother's couch, wiggling my toes all night long. I was so full of excitement and hopped up on caffeine, I don't think I slept a wink.

What would life had been like had I not acted on faith and made the move out west? I'm not sure, I suspect not nearly as exciting or professionally stimulating as it's been.

The story has a funny twist that's also about taking action. Remember those credit cards I used to fund my exodus from Ontario? They caught up to me. In fact, they caught up and buried me. After only three months in Vancouver, I was beginning to do well, but could barely manage the interest on all the debt I was carrying. When I tallied up all my outstanding debt, including a student loan and car payments, I was horrified to discover I owed almost $30,000. That was a little less than I planned to make in an entire year. I was stricken with fear. I didn't know what to do. I couldn't afford to pay the accumulating interest and needed to find a solution. The phone began to ring and my creditors wanted their payments.

I approached this challenge with two lines of thought. I looked at what was best for me and what was best for my creditors. When I evaluated what was best for me, the only option was to declare bankruptcy. When I look at what was best for everyone, I had a twinge of guilt and a little voice that said, "You really should try to pay your debt." I chose to pay it back. I engaged a local company that specialized in this sort of thing and we set up a program of repayment. I wasn't crazy about the $700 per month payments, but I knew it was my only choice.

For me, all four Schuller components were there in this scenario. I had started to play and dream about this move to Vancouver. I had begun to pray for a safe passage and transition in my new home. I had planned to stay. This move was one of the biggest commitments I had ever made. But now it was time to pay. I knew I had to pay. I wasn't happy about the idea of repaying $700 per month for the next 42 months, but I knew it was my only choice. I had decided long ago that I was going to lead my new life with character and integrity. That meant taking responsibility for my actions and my debt.

I wasn't done paying the price even after the last installment was done. What they neglected to tell me was that my credit would be harshly affected by these derogatory marks on my history. Even though I paid the debt off quicker than expected, I still had trouble with my credit for the following four years.

Taking action by moving out west was an easy decision to make and follow through on; it was a fun, exciting adventure. Facing the consequences and preparing to pay off 30K in debt was a little harder. Today, my credit has been completely restored. It took some time, but I'm glad I did it the way I did. It taught me about having to make hard, uncomfortable decisions.

Today, I understand a few things about success and failure. I know that failure is much more work than success. I have to tell you that living on the street, as a drop out loser, was much harder than the life I have today. Every day was a struggle; every day was a fight for survival.

Living in conflict with your dreams and true character will eat you up inside. For years, I knew that deep inside, I was a good person who had valid hopes and dreams. Yet every day I woke up, I lived in conflict with my inner self. A long time ago, a friend of mine told me that he thought a lot of human misery comes from people knowing what they want and who they are, but not doing anything in the present to fulfill it. I'm not sure about anybody else, but it sure rang true for me.

Our days are filled with all kinds of things and events. Some of which serve us well and others are just time burglars. With my Life Manifesto in front of me each week, I can clearly allocate time to events that help me slowly fulfill the life I want to live. It all comes down to taking an active role in your future.

Action is the only thing that counts, once you've planned and committed yourself. In fact, everything else is just happy talk until you begin. Words like love, success, gratitude and charity have nice meanings. Until they are acted upon, their residence is with Webster, not the world around us. They simply represent a meaning or concept, but don't really count for much.
Now acting upon love for your neighbor, community or family member, is entirely different. Here we see the concept brought to life supported with hard evidence of its existence through action. Your behavior and your life embrace the essence when you begin to live these spiritual ideals.

I hear people tell me they're so grateful. I think to myself, prove it! Don't tell me, show me! Gratitude isn't just a feeling; it's a tangible, outward display of gratefulness. It's not just supposed to be a warm and fuzzy feeling you keep inside. It's supposed to motivate you to share with others.

Then there's success. You cannot hoard success. You cannot transfer it, yet it can be shared. Success is not permanent; today's success may be tomorrow's failure. Change is the constant for the race always is being run. Success cannot be rested upon, thought about complacently, or purchased through mail order. Success is an ideal that comes from your paradigms. Defined, it is as varied as the 5.6 billion people on planet Earth. The dictionary says this, "The achievement of something desired, planned, or attempted."

I like Napoleon Hill's example:

"It is literally true that you can succeed best and quickest by helping others to succeed."

Success is what you believe it to be, but always involves action and movement. Arriving successful is like the end of a race, for spectators leave soon thereafter and you are staring at the empty bleachers. I describe success as giving, loving, caring and helping. Sharing your good fortune with those in need. Living each day successfully includes service to self, to family and to community. It includes constant work and attention. And it is worth the labor for the nectar is sweet and the view spectacular.

Nothing happens by accident. Successful people are not born, they are made. The same holds true for successful businesses and careers. In our cookie cutter world of quick fixes and fast cures, one thing will remain constant and that's the law of reciprocity. That one set of actions produces a certain result. Imagine eating poorly for years and expecting some mail order abs-thingy to have you looking like the model in just three weeks and four easy installments. Not true, yet the society we live in breeds this mentality.

What happened to the good old fashion work ethic? Imagine a farmer who squanders his profits from the past year's harvest. He does not effectively plan and budget for seed purchase in the spring. Spring rolls around and the farmer is too busy or too lazy to solve his seed dilemma. Spring turns to summer, with still no action. Finally, the harvest months arrive and the farmer realizes he missed his opportunity to cultivate crops that year. Imagine such a farmer realizing his mistake, kneeling in his fields praying for God to please give him some crops this year. If you do, I promise to plant next year.

Sorry chum, but that's not how it works. Seeds planted today reap the harvests of tomorrow. It's the law. A law that no self will can maneuver around. Knowing this, I will continue plant, sow and reap, because that's the way it's worked since the beginning of time. Lights Camera *Action!* Dress rehearsal is over.

7 Questions:

1. How will acting on your dreams change things for you?

2. What bank checks or lottery tickets have you neglected to cash?

3. If you knew sand would turn to diamonds, how much sand would you pack?

4. Are you free? Do your actions reflect this freedom?

5. If you were to reach into your pocket today, what would you discover that you have possessed for years?

6. What tough action decisions are you facing?

7. Will you act on the things most important in your life or will you be like the careless farmer?

If God had a refrigerator, your face would be on it.

SECRET *6*

Who's Driving *your* Bus?

W hen I was at the lowest point in life, I remember my simple prayer. **God help me.** He did, and today, I know that just a tiny sprinkling of God's blessing can last a lifetime.

If you are closed to matters of faith and a higher power's existence or cannot, for whatever reason, find yourself to believe in such things, this chapter may or may not help you. I do not intend to discuss in great deal what God is or any other deep matters regarding religion, theology or psychology. If you are struggling to understand and define your faith, I suggest C. S. Lewis. For now, I will assume you believe in something. And whether you have an ounce or a ton of faith, this chapter will indeed speak to your heart.

Today, I have a "faith life." My faith expands and retracts, depending on the time I give to spiritual exercise. Every day, I get up and think about this verse and it really motivates me:

Do you not know that those who run in a race all run, but only one receives the prize? Run in such a way that you may win.

1 Corinthians 9:24

I want to win; I've always been a competitor. When I get up tomorrow, I will tackle the day with a champion's spirit, looking to conquer the market place for my company, deliver the best speaking programs for my clients, and be the best father and husband to my family. Why? Because I know it's possible, for anything I believe, I know I can achieve.

Where does this confidence come from? It comes from my faith. Not just faith in God, but faith in myself, faith in my company, faith in people. Faith in my personal destiny. The reason "why" has been sufficiently answered in my life. My only job now is to walk in faith each day, looking for opportunities to fulfill that destiny. After all, what else can I believe in? I've personally witnessed in my short lifetime more miracles than recorded in the New Testament. I am a miracle, considering the road I traveled. I should have been dead in the 1980s, but somehow I survived.

We should not be alarmed; most of us have had these spiritual encounters in our life. That is why I have very little problem believing in something greater than myself. I have no problem surrendering to this power, as it was this very power that cared for me when I was unable to care for myself. Today, I just know this power is real. If you don't believe me, ask me again and I'll tell you. I used to say, "If I can see the goodness of the Lord in the land of the living, I will believe. Every day, I wake up and go out into this world I witness first hand the goodness of the Lord in the land of the living…and I do believe!

This next story I like, because it captures the strength and essence of what true faith is like. This is a wonderful story of hope.

You see, there was this pastor in Brooklyn, New York who recently had taken over a new parish. He was fresh from Seminary College and his job was to rebuild this urban church community. When he arrived at the church, he was quite discouraged. The church was very run down, it had graffiti on the walls, some of the windows were broken, and it definitely needed a paint job. The young preacher wasn't discouraged; he got some volunteers and began in early October restoring this wonderful little community church. His goal was to have his first service on Christmas Eve. Things were going well until, about three days before Christmas Eve, there was a terrible rainstorm in the New York area. The rain seeped into the church through the walls and the leaky roof. When the preacher showed up one morning, he noticed a large piece of plaster had fallen from behind the altar. He was quite discouraged and heartbroken, but he began cleaning the mess right away.

Later, he was on his way downtown when he noticed a rummage sale for charity and he decided to support their cause. He was going through some old boxes when he found a beautiful handmade tablecloth. As he pulled it out of the box, he noticed it was very old and yellow with age. He held the tablecloth up, it was about five feet wide and ten feet long — it was the perfect size to cover up the hole above the altar. He offered them a fair price and made his way back to his church. As he approached the church steps, he noticed an old lady waiting at the bus stop. By now, the rain had turned to snow. He knew there wasn't another bus due for at least an hour, so he invited the old woman in for a warm cup of tea and they began to chat.

As the pastor went up the stepladder to hang his newly purchased tablecloth, he turned around and noticed that the old woman sitting in the front pew had a strange look on her face. In fact, her complexion had turned completely white. He asked her what was the problem, and she said to him, "Pastor, 35 years ago, I lived in Austria and the Great War broke out. My husband and I were captured. I was sent to a work camp and my husband was sent to a concentration camp. We never saw each other again. That tablecloth you're hanging today looks just like the one my mother and I handmade the Christmas before the war broke out. Tell me pastor, in the bottom right hand corner, does it have the initials, 'RGB?'" The pastor reached down, held the tablecloth up and to his amazement, there were the initials, "RGB." The pastor was tremendously moved. He took the tablecloth down and offered it to the old woman but she said, "No, it belongs here in your church."

They talked late into the night about how, over such a vast amount of time and great distance, this table cloth had united this woman and this pastor. The woman had admitted that she had never lost hope and that one day she knew she would be reunited with her husband. The pastor wanted to give her something and the only thing he could think of was a ride home, so he walked her to his car and they drove off to her house in South Queens.

Two days later, it was Christmas Eve — a beautifully joyous evening. Many people from the community came and sang Christmas carols. It was truly a blessed night. Afterwards, people came up, shook the pastor's hand, and told him how they enjoyed the service and that they would be joining him on a weekly basis. As the pastor was closing up, he noticed one man still there. He walked to the back of the church where the little old man was sitting in the pew. He was staring aimlessly at the tablecloth hanging above the altar.

As the pastor turned to the man, he noticed that his face had turned completely white. He asked if he could help him. The old fellow said, "Pastor, 35 years ago, I lived in Austria and the Great War broke out. My wife and I were captured. I went to a concentration camp while she went to a work camp. I haven't seen her since. As I look at this tablecloth today, I'm reminded of the hope that I never lost. Pastor, that tablecloth above your altar looks just like the one my wife and her mother made the year before the war broke out. Tell me pastor, does it have the initials, 'RGB' in the bottom right-hand corner"? The pastor was speechless. Tears began to stream down his face. He grabbed the little old man, helped him into his car and headed toward South Queens. That evening, the little old man and the little old lady were reunited after being apart for more than three decades.

I am told that this story is   true; I don't really know for sure. What I do know is that it gives me hope and faith to carry on, even when things look bleak. It teaches me that life is very precious and regardless of my lack of understanding, I must trust that a greater power always is at work in my best interest, helping me create a life that is much better than anything I could possibly imagine.

In 1988, while living on Vancouver's skid row, I was penniless, homeless and for the most part, hopeless. I never believed my life could end up in such a mess. As a child, I fooled around with alcohol and drugs but never imagined it would lead to this. I don't ever remember sitting in my career studies course saying, "When I grow up, I want to be a junkie loser." But that's precisely what happened.

I rebelled against my parents and figures of authority. I desperately wanted to be accepted and liked by people, so I began hanging out with street kids and my behavior reflected this. Before I was 16, I had been in trouble with the police and had gone as far as to experiment with every kind of drug out there, including the use of needles. I was willing to do whatever it took to fit in and be accepted by others that I ended up "selling my soul for rock and roll." I knew right from wrong; I simply made the wrong choices. I paid for it for more than 10 years. By the time I was in my early 20s, I was unrecognizable to most who knew me when I was young. I had a serious cocaine and heroin addiction and I was homeless. I hustled the streets and did what I could to survive. I used to sleep under the Georgia Street viaduct in Vancouver, because there's an industrial steam pipe running through there. It was warm and dry. Many street people used to live there.

As an active drug addict and street person, I witnessed many terribly tragic events. I watched good friends die and commit suicide. I watched others fall prey to the sex trade. I witnessed poverty, homelessness, desperation and despair. I watched, as scores of people poisoned themselves, and contracted incurable diseases. I watched crime take over Vancouver and a small slum grow to gain international notoriety. But amazingly, in the end, I watched myself leave that hell that I called my life. I don't know why I was allowed to walk through the shadow of death and come out unharmed. I hope that in the end, this one mystery will be revealed to me.

The day was Dec. 25th, 1988. I had no money, no place to be. It was a sad day indeed and I was hungry. I had slept most of the day away and when I awoke, most of the free shelter food and soup lines had packed up and were gone. I could feel my tight little belly grumbling for something, but had no idea what I was going to do. As I walked down the boulevard, I noticed how empty the streets were. Christmas time is lonely when you're a bum. The street action was quiet; most people had a place to be — at least for a day or two — through the holidays. I was happy for them, but looked forward to when things got back to normal again. When you live your life with as much regret as I did, Christmas was a suicide season. It was the one time each year when I really felt like I could pull it off. Santa never came to our bridge and life sucked!

The longer I was awake, the hungrier I became. I decided that I deserved to eat like anyone else and as I thought about this more, I got really angry. I spotted a convenience store on the corner and decided I was going to do something bold. Being a thief wasn't my normal style, but on this day I would make an exception to quiet my rumbling belly and subside my indignant anger. I walked into the store trying to act as casual and inconspicuous as possible. I headed for the back fridge and grabbed some pepperoni and cheese. I stuffed them under my jacket and with my heart pounding, I headed for the door. I had almost reached the door, when the man at the till said, "Wait a minute." He looked into my eyes and knew I was afraid. He also new darn well that I was not checking price tags in the back of this store. I could feel the sweat building on my head and neck, when something special happened. The man came from behind the counter and opened the door for me. As I walked out of the store, he touched my shoulder and said to me, "You have a Merry Christmas, sir."

As I walked down the street eating my "hot" and spicy pepperoni sticks, tears welled up in my eyes and all I could think of was that he called me "sir." Imagine that, calling ME "SIR."

Several months later, I became very ill from living outside and in November 1989, my mother visited me from Ontario and took me back home to live with her. When we got on the plane that day, I knew that I would never see Vancouver this way again. And thanks be to God, I never have. My recovery and abstinence began on July 26th, 1991, and since that day, I have no need to get drunk or high. That little prayer I said on that street carried me a long way. As my recovery grows, so does my faith. It's impossible for me not to believe in something bigger than me. What happened to me, really helped me understand two things about God and faith:

One: There is a God and I'm not him.

Two: If this God saved me from the street, what have I got to fear in life?

Fast forward to Dec. 26th, 2001. I had been complaining to my wife about stomach cramps, so I went to lie down. The pain did not subside, but worsened. By evening, it was time to visit a hospital. I arrived at Burnaby General around 8 pm. It was rather quiet and I was able to see a doctor right away. Without a detailed diagnosis, I was given some pain medication and sent home. The medication took the pain away and I was able to sleep. The medications ran out, but the pain remained and by New Year's Eve, I was one sick puppy. Back to the hospital I went and this time they kept me.

The following day, I was diagnosed with acute diverticulitis. I had also acquired a nasty abdominal infection called peritonitis. Twenty years ago, peritonitis just killed you. It's the type of infection that only high-test antibiotics can fight. I was rotting from the inside out. Diverticulitis is a lower colon disorder that weakens the colon, causing it to leak internally. The peritonitis is caused by the body having to deal with these toxins behind the abdominal wall.

They tried to fight my infection with antibiotics, but nothing was working. On Jan. 5th, I went in for surgery number one; by Jan. 7th, I was rushed in for a second surgery. On Jan. 12th, I went in the third time, and again, a week later, the fourth major surgery. In less than two weeks, I underwent four major life-threatening surgeries.

The reason for all the additional surgeries was caused by something called "MRSA," a super bug that caused my body to reject all normal antibiotics. I was not able to heal and was literally dying in front of my family, the surgeon and the hospital staff. Once they figured out what was really going on, I was stabilized and began to heal. For more than three weeks, I was in critical care. Many days, they weren't sure what was to become of old Joe Roberts.

In my time in the hospital, I became very close to my family, my mom, my wife, and my friends. When I was lying in that hospital bed with every kind of tube and needle poking in and out of me, the only things that mattered were my friends, my family and my faith. After all I'd been through, you would think I would automatically get it, but I didn't. It took me three weeks of crying, praying, begging, bargaining, wheeling and dealing, for me to finally surrender and have faith.

I was listening to some great music by Van Morrison when I heard the message. The message was that I was going to be fine, my family was going to be fine and everyone was going to be fine, because He's in charge. Not Van Morrison, but

God. Until I let that burden go, I was a mess. I can't, nor do I ever want to walk another day without faith. I can't imagine what the world looks like to an individual that has nothing to believe or hope for. When I transferred my life and will to the care of this Higher Power, I felt great relief.

Throughout my entire ordeal, I lost 60 pounds, was hospitalized for more than seven weeks, and spent another seven at home in bed. I realized that once again, this faith of mine had protected me and walked me through one more time. They say that every time one door closes, another one opens. They didn't tell me about the hell of standing in the hallway.

Many times, God will allow a painful situation or circumstance to "swallow us up." This season in our spiritual growth is simply a holding pattern. We can't move to the left or the right. All we can do is sit, like Jonah sat in the belly of that great fish, so God can have our undivided attention and speak to us.

God put Jonah in a holding pattern because He needed to speak to his heart. Jonah was all alone. There were no friends to call, no colleagues to drop by, no books to read, no food to eat, no interference, and no interruptions. He had plenty of time to sit, think, meditate, and pray. When we're deep down in the midst of a difficult situation, God can talk to us. When He has our undivided attention, He can show us things about ourselves that we might not otherwise see.

A Few Of God's Holding Patterns:

When you are sick in your physical body and you have prayed, but God has not healed you yet, you are in a holding pattern.

When you are having problems with your children and you have put them on the altar, but God has not delivered them yet, you are in a holding pattern.

When you are in a broken relationship and you have given it over to God, but it has not been restored yet, you are in a holding pattern.

When the doors slam shut before you can knock on them, you are in a holding pattern.

When we are deep in the belly of a difficult situation, there are no interruptions. God has our undivided attention. All we can do is sit, think, meditate, and pray. We cannot run from God, because there are no mountains that are high enough, valleys that are low enough, rivers that are wide enough, rooms that are dark enough, or places that are hidden enough.

We must remember to praise Him while we're waiting and remember three things:

The pattern has a purpose.

The pattern has a plan.

The pattern has a process.

So stop struggling and start listening, praying and trusting. He'll keep you right where you are until you can clearly hear Him say, "I love you."

A Prayer:

"Father, forgive my unbelief. I know you love me and will turn anything around to benefit me. You have planned nothing for me but victories and I am ready to receive them, regardless of how difficult the path. Amen."

The shortest distance between a problem and a solution is the distance between your knees and the floor. The one who kneels to the Lord can stand up to anything.

A Positive Thought:

If God had a refrigerator, your picture would be on it. If He had a wallet, your photo would be in it. He sends you flowers every spring and a sunrise every morning. Whenever you want to talk, He'll listen. He can live anywhere in the universe, and He chose your heart. Face it — He's crazy about you.

After I had been clean awhile I came across this poem, which for me, said it all. It's a poem by Margaret Fishback Powers:

FOOTPRINTS

By Margaret Powers

One night a man had a dream. He dreamed he was walking along the beach with the LORD. Across the sky flashed scenes from his life. For each scene he noticed two sets of footprints in the sand: one belonging to him, and the other to the LORD. When the last scene of his life flashed before him, he looked back at the footprints in the sand. He noticed that many times along the path of his life there was only one set of footprints. He also noticed that it happened at the very lowest and saddest times in his life. This really bothered him and he questioned the LORD about it: "LORD, you said that once I decided to follow you, you'd walk with me all the way. But I have noticed that during the most troublesome times in my life, there is only one set of footprints. I don't understand why when I needed you most you would leave me." The LORD replied, "My son, my precious child, I love you and I would never leave you. During your times of trial and suffering, when you see only one set of footprints, it was then that I carried you."

No matter how intense spiritual experiences are in my life, I still can get distracted. That's why it's very important for me to feed my spiritual life. It's like going to the gym for your soul. If you never exercise your faith, you are likely never to expand it. Today I try to find time every day for reading and prayer. It strengthens my faith and allows me to enter into a complex world with assurance and confidence from a divine source.

So how does faith line up with living your dreams and goals?

Let me share with you one of the most positive revelations I have discovered. Every person has a road to walk and a destiny to fulfill. But what makes us unique? We all seem to want and desire different things. Some people want to raise healthy, happy children, where another might want to succeed in the business world. One person wants to fly airplanes and another wants to become an Olympian. One wants to learn Spanish, while someone else wants to travel to Australia to study marine biology. Why do we each want what we want? What drives us to desire and long for these experiences? Why does something that really gets me excited not have the same effect on you?

I think I know why and it's the most exciting thing I have come across, as it has everything to do with faith. What if what you want didn't really come from your mind? What if what you want is sent to you or given to you by some sort of spiritual incubation? What if the God of your understanding said before you were born, this is my plan for so and so?

The old scripture says that God knows every hair on our head. Is he also responsible for what we desire and really love? Could what we really want out of life simply be God's will for us? I know this — when I'm doing what I REALLY love, I'm most connected with the world around me and I'm most happy. That's when I'm totally at peace with the world. And that's when I feel connected to my Higher Power.

So, what if this is true? That what we really desire out of life — our deepest and most intimate longings – really are our Higher Power's will for our lives? We have seen great lives in the past transform out of what seemed unlikely odds and yet they all say the same thing. "I just knew this is what I was supposed to do with my life." It's my passion, my fate, my work, my destiny, and my life. What are you supposed to do?

Now comes the dynamite of this thought. If it's true, that what you want to really accomplish in life is aligned with what God wants, and what the universe has already predetermined, how can you possibly fail? How can you fail at this – it's what you've been destined for? It's your birthright. Can you imagine, you cannot and will not fail? Nothing on this planet can stop you, because you have the ultimate mentor believing you can do it. If you stumble, he will pick you up, if you become discouraged, he will send someone to inspire. Your only job is to exercise the free will you were given and begin to move toward your dreams. But I guarantee you that you won't be doing it alone. No sir, you have — and always will have — an angel watching over you, making sure that you do not fail.

It's time we accept our victory and begin living like we are free to succeed and prosper. Love and live more abundantly is the promise. With God before me, who can be against me?

You've already won!

When I think about a life well lived, I think about that person's legacy. I think about, not just my life, but also the lives before and mostly the lives after I die. We live in a world that teaches us to have a limited time frame for our work and the contribution we make. We tend to think within the time that is "ours" and not much further. Besides your last will and testament, what other plans do you have for your life once you pass from this world? What legacy do you intend to leave behind? What impact or contributions do you want to make to this world? Forget about Freedom 55. How about freedom 505? What impact do you want your life to have 500 years from now?

Thinking like this is not normal. It's a little strange to be thinking about contributions I can make to the world hundreds of years after my life has ended. How can you touch the world so far into the future? It's easy. Do you have children? Will they have children, will their children have children, and grandchildren and great grandchildren? It reminds you of the old shampoo commercial. Whether we like it or not, we will have an impact on the generations that follow. What we do today can have a tremendous effect. You may say, "I don't have children and never intend to." That's fine, but do you teach something, are you involved with other people, are you at all planting your seed, because if you are, then I guarantee you that you will touch someone's life in your time on this planet. No man is an island. No woman is either.

In my life, there have been many people who have helped me on my journey. Too many to write about in this chapter. But two incidents jump to mind when I think about the impact others have had on my life and they both involve matters of faith.

When I finally hit bottom, I went through a week that was pure hell. Not just for me, but also for my mother, who fought to keep me alive. It involved four ambulance rides, two hospitalizations, three emergency wards, one psychiatric hospital, a five-point restraint experience, heart failure, respiratory failure and two emergency code blues. I had lost all control and today, I only have vague recollections of the events that took place that week in May 1991. I was very ill and at death's door. My mom was there for the whole ride. But by the time she drove me from Barrie to Toronto, she was exhausted. Trying to enter me into a recovery center, she was refused because I was quite intoxicated. They told her I would have to return the next day and to take me to the hospital were I could begin to detoxify. When we reached Toronto Western Hospital, I began to slide in and out of consciousness. In this state of overdose, they were afraid I was going to fall asleep and slip in a coma. They were slapping my face, trying to keep me awake. Not really understanding what was going on, I began to fight back tossing a few staff members around before the hospital goons pinned me to the table in what is called five-point restraint. There was a 3-inch thick, leather strap belted down across both my hands and feet, with a large strap running across my forehead so I wouldn't bang my head. They had stripped me of my clothes and left me alone in this cold room.

My mother was distraught and frightened. She had reached the end of her threshold and broke down and cried in the hospital waiting area. While she was crying, a woman came to comfort her and asked why she was so upset. She told the woman that she thought her son was going to die and that there was nothing she could do. The wise woman said there was something they could do. They could pray and have faith. The woman prayed with my mother a while and before she left, she promised my mom that her prayer group would say a special prayer for me at their meeting the next day.

I never met this woman or any of her group. My mother never saw the woman again. The next day, things began to change for me. It was the exact same situation as when I was ill in the hospital later in life. The prayer warriors from my church had me in their thoughts.

Do I believe in prayer? You betcha. It's one of the best exercises to grow your faith. Does prayer work? You bet it does. Even the most cynical scientists have admitted that prayer, as mysterious as it is to them, has helped many cases which otherwise seemed hopeless. I know I was a hopeless case. Having these good ladies pray for me is what I believed contributed to my healing and the dawn of my new life. Why did these people come into my life at that time? I may never know. But I will continue to believe that things come together in perfect timing. And that people join our lives for specific reasons, even if we can't see it at the time.

The second faith encounter I had was again in Ontario a little while after I moved back to live with my mother. I did not get clean right away. I still had some learning to do before I finally quit for good. During this time, I got into some serious trouble. I found myself facing some serious legal issues and my life looked very bleak. During this time, I met a cop. I hated cops. They were the enemy, I wished ill on anybody that had anything to do with law enforcement.

The cop I met was Scott MacLeod of the Barrie OPP. When we met, my life was a real mess. Drugs had taken their toll and I was not likely to live much longer if something didn't change. Scott and I met while he was tending to official police business. Unfortunately for me, I was that business. I remember him talking to me like I was a normal person. He treated me with respect and dignity.

When Scott and I met, I was barricaded in the basement of my mother's house with a 9-millimeter pistol aimed to blow my head off. He was in charge of talking to me and making sure I didn't do anything rash. In many respects, I owe my life to Scott. He walked me through a really tough day back in the spring of '91. But his caring for me went further. You see, when I was arrested Scott had a choice to make. He could pursue a number of other charges (I was in possession of a bag full of prescription pills), or he could simply pursue the weapons charge. If he pursued the weapons charge, I had a better chance of getting my life back together. With my history, it was a much better alternative than a dozen or more drug offenses.

Scott gave me a break. Just at the right time, too. It was this break that began a series of events that turned my life around. At 10 years clean and sober, I returned to Ontario to celebrate with friends I had made earlier in recovery. When I went to Barrie, I gave Scott my 10-year medallion from my support group. I told him he helped me earn it and that I was so grateful we crossed paths. He told me something very moving that day. He told me that he became a cop to make a difference in the world. He had high ideals when he started his career, but the job is a tough one. Every day, all he saw was the ugly side of life. He told me that's why a lot of cops get discouraged. After I got clean, I stayed in touch with Scott and periodically kept him up-to-date on my progress. I wrote him a letter telling him the effect he had on my life. I told him when I graduated from college, when I got married, when I won awards. I kept him informed on the investment he had made in me a long time ago.

Scott reached his twentieth year milestone as a cop and was awarded a Meritorious Service Medal. He was asked to give a short speech on what being an officer of the law meant to him. Scott told the story of how we had met and the difference he had made in my life and that of my family.

Imagine!! Scott led his life with the faith that being a cop was a good thing. Something noble and true. Facing danger every day, trying to make the world a better place to be, seldom being recognized for his courage. Today, I work with the police. Most times, they're my friends (except the ones that write me traffic tickets). All my life, I saw cops as the enemy and ironically, it was a cop who saved my sorry butt. Imagine!

How has someone touched your life? What spiritual or mysterious events have you experienced but cannot explain? We all have a story of how someone impacted our lives. The next story, author unknown, is one of my favorites.

One day, when I was a freshman in high school, I saw a kid from my class was walking home from school. His name was Kyle. It looked like he was carrying all of his books. I thought to myself, "Why would anyone bring home all his books on a Friday? He must really be a nerd." I had quite a weekend planned (parties and a football game with my friends tomorrow afternoon), so I shrugged my shoulders and went on. As I was walking, I saw a bunch of kids running toward him. They ran at him, knocking all his books out of his arms and tripping him so he landed in the dirt. His glasses went flying, and I saw them land in the grass about 10 feet from him. He looked up and I saw this terrible sadness in his eyes. My heart went out to him. So, I jogged over to him and as he crawled around looking for his glasses, I saw a tear in his eye. As I handed him his glasses, I said, "Those guys are jerks. They really should get lives." He looked at me and said, "Hey thanks!" There was a big smile on his face. It was one of those smiles that showed real gratitude.

I helped him pick up his books, and asked him where he lived. As it turned out, he lived near me, so I asked him why I had never seen him before. He said he had gone to a private school before now. I would have never hung out with a private school kid. We talked all the way home, and I carried some of his books. He turned out to be a pretty cool kid. I asked him if he wanted to play a little football with my friends. He said yes. We hung out all weekend and the more I got to know Kyle, the more I liked him, and my friends thought the same of him. Monday morning came, and there was Kyle with the huge stack of books again. I stopped him and said, "Boy, you are going to really build some serious muscles with this pile of books everyday!" He just laughed and handed me half the books. Over the next four years, Kyle and I became best friends. When we were seniors, we began to think about college. Kyle decided on Georgetown, and I was going to Duke. I knew that we would always be friends, that the miles would never be a problem. He was going to be a doctor, and I was going for business on a football scholarship. Kyle was valedictorian of our class. I teased him all the time about being a nerd. He had to prepare a speech for graduation.

I was so glad it wasn't me having to get up there and speak. Graduation day, I saw Kyle. He looked great. He was one of those guys that really found himself during high school. He filled out and actually looked good in glasses. He had more dates than I had and all the girls loved him. Boy, sometimes I was jealous. Today was one of those days. I could see that he was nervous about his speech. So, I smacked him on the back and said, "Hey, big guy, you'll be great!" He looked at me with one of those looks (the really grateful one) and smiled. "Thanks," he said.

As he started his speech, he cleared his throat, and began. "Graduation is a time to thank those who helped you make it through those tough years. Your parents, your teachers, your siblings, maybe a coach, but mostly your friends. I am here to tell all of you that being a friend to someone is the best gift you can give them. I am going to tell you a story." I just looked at my friend with disbelief as he told the story of the first day we met. He had planned to kill himself over the weekend. He talked of how he had cleaned out his locker so his Mom wouldn't have to do
it later and was carrying his stuff home. He looked hard at me and gave me a little smile. "Thankfully, I was saved. My friend saved me from doing the unspeakable." I heard the gasp go through the crowd as this handsome, popular boy told us all about his weakest moment. I saw his Mom and Dad looking at me and smiling that same grateful smile. Not until that moment, did I realize its depth.

Never underestimate the power of your actions. With one small gesture, you can change a person's life.

God puts us all in each other's lives to impact one another in some way. An event very similar to the one above happened to me personally one day. I have a good friend that I've known for more than five years. One day at a convention in Wisconsin, he began to share his story. He told those in the audience that five years before, he was about to throw his live away. He was tired of working and seeing no results and had made a decision to throw it all out the window. He was about to leave his house when the phone rang. He talked to this friend for an hour and after that phone call, he didn't feel so sure about his decision to ruin his life. He told people that day it was me who had called him. I was completely shocked. Why had I not heard his story before? I asked him why hadn't he told me this story before? He explained that we each get our chance to change the world for better and that it wasn't really necessary for me to know. He told me that he loved me and was glad that I was in his life. He also told me that I shouldn't try and take credit for his success, because it was really God who called him. I was just a willing participant. My friend is a deeply spiritual guy today. One whose faith and humility I respect.

Today, I know that my life sometimes has more to do with other people's lives than it has to do with me. I still don't really understand God's timing or his funky way of doing things and why should I? I'm just a mere man. In fact, how dare I even question the mind or character of the creator of the universe? It's none of my business how he runs things. I need to remember that I play but a small part in the big picture. I'm no star. I'm just a humble man seeking safe passage on this journey through life. Any good I can do along the way, I shall. All I need to do is walk by faith.

My faith has been tested. You truly get to know what faith really is when it's all you're holding on to. For those who still struggle with faith, try this for now: believe that I believe. Start here and pray for knowledge and wisdom to be revealed to you.

Today, I know that faith is not belief without proof, but rather trust without reservations.

7 Questions:

1. How has your faith helped you to succeed?

2. How has your faith helped others?

3. What spiritual exercises do you use to strengthen your faith?

4. During times of despair, how has faith sustained you?

5. What can faith help you leave behind for the next generation?

6. Some problems have no immediate solutions. How can faith help?

7. How has the faith of someone else shaped or guided your life?

7

"The men who hold high places must be the one's to start to mold a new reality closer to the heart." -Getty Lee, Musician

SECRET 7

Becoming a Hero *in the* Age of Celebrities

How many apples are in a seed? This question is profound when you think about it. Many variables come into play. The answer could be unlimited or none, depending on the farmer, the soil, the earth and how that seed is nurtured. Each one of us has the opportunity to reap an abundant harvest from our orchards of life. In doing so, we can become a hero. But the call of the day seems to be for celebrities, not farmers.

Every day, the media, the television and the newspapers are displaying images of "would be" celebrities. Some are simply grabbing onto their Andy Warhol appointed 15 minutes of fame; others enjoy the limelight for some time. I remember a seminar my friend, Tom Howse, gave entitled, "Becoming a Hero in the Age of Celebrities," and I thought it was fitting for the title of this chapter. I thought deep about what Tom had to say and the more I listened, the more I began to think about the true heroes that have mentored me and taught me my greatest lessons.

He asked us if we could recite the winning teams of the last three Super Bowl Games, the Stanley Cup or the World Series. He asked us who won the last Academy Award or even the Time Life person of the year three years ago. Tom's point was this. We won't remember the names of the famous, but we will remember the names of our heroes. Those people planted a seed in us. Think back to the teachers that had the greatest effect on your life. That special coach you may have had. The camp leader, or maybe a youth pastor. The person who taught you one of your most valuable lessons. Or the person who was there for you when you needed them most. His lesson seemed to beg the question. How many apples are in your seed?

When I was a young teenager, I had the opportunity to meet my greatest hero. He wasn't my greatest hero at the time, but his story and his personal impact on me will last forever. They say it takes a minute to find a special person, an hour to appreciate them, a day to love them, and an entire life to appreciate them.

I grew up in a media family. My grandfather owned CKMP radio station in Midland Ontario and my mother and her four younger brothers had grown up in the broadcasting industry. As it was, we often were at the heart of many large — and not so large — media events in the city. One particular Saturday morning, I was dragged off to what I thought was going to be another boring PR event and I reluctantly went along after some preliminary complaining. I soon found myself at

Centennial Park in downtown Barrie, Ontario. The local radio
and TV station hosted the event. There was a buzz in the air
that day as we all stood waiting in anticipation of our guest's
arrival. I don't remember if it was morning or afternoon, but I
remember glancing down the road and sure enough, he was
about to arrive. We could see him and a large gathering of
people headed toward the stage that was set up for this special
visit.

As he got closer, I decided I wanted to get an autograph. The
man wasn't that famous yet, but I had a feeling that one day,
people might remember what this guy was doing. As he
approached the stage, I nudged my little body in front and
asked him for his autograph. He smiled at me, rubbed my hair
into a mess, and gladly obliged my adolescent request. As he
took the stage and began to speak, I could see he was tired.
Yet, through his fatigue, he managed to say something that
sparked the hearts of those around me as the crowd exploded
with enthusiasm and cheers. He talked about his life's
mission, he talked about his commitment, and he talked about
how his adversity had driven him to succeed even more. He
spoke with passion, with direction and with heart. No sooner
had he spoken, he left the stage and continued on the long
run, which is his legacy today. The man that touched me that
day was Terry Fox. By the time Terry was done, he had
touched the heart of every Canadian. His goal was simple, yet
huge. Terry wanted to raise one dollar from every Canadian
for cancer research.

When Terry passed through Barrie, he still was somewhat
unknown. When his journey came to a halt just outside
Thunder Bay, Ontario, Terry was known by everyone. As a
young man, I was touched by his courage. Here's a guy who
had every reason in the world to give up, but he didn't. Here's

a guy that against all odds, tried anyway. Terry had it all. He learned to profit from his adversity, he learned to overcome his fear, and he learned to build a Trinity of Success by writing his goal, committing to his goal, and taking action on his goal. Terry had tremendous faith in the people of Canada and he was not let down. By February 1981, he achieved his goal of 24.17 million dollars. Terry died in June 1981 at the age of 22. To date, The Terry Fox Foundation has raised more than 300 million dollars for cancer research.

When I have bad days, as we all do, I think of Terry Fox and the lessons he taught me as a child. I reflect back on the day we met and the autograph he gave me. But what is more, is the imprint he left on my soul.

In the 12-step fellowship, we have a prayer we use call the Serenity Prayer. It goes like this:

God grant me the serenity

To accept the things I cannot change,

The courage to change the things I can,

And the wisdom to know the difference.

Terry Fox taught me about the courage to change the things I can! He planted many seeds in his life and the fruit of his work will continue to produce for years to come.

For me, life is about trying to be a hero today. I took from my community for many years and today I feel it's my duty to give back, since I have been so blessed. A hero is someone who gives, not because they're asked, but because it's the right thing to do. Why do I want to be a hero in life? Simple. I would rather be selfless and happy, helping people than anything else. I have found that life is profoundly better when you're helping other people by sharing your talents and gifts. I remember a conversation I once overheard regarding the wealth of the Rockefeller family. They asked, "How much money do you figure he left when he died?" A wise man in the back said "all of it." What is wealth that is not shared? What is wisdom, if not passed on? How will the world get to be a better place if we don't plant our seeds today?

When I was in grade one, I would go to my Grandma's for lunch. Our school was at the end of a long road and my Grandma's house was close by. All I had to do was follow a trail through the forest to Grandma's house. I also owned a bright red rain jacket, but that's where the similarities end.

Each day, I would go to Grandma's. I loved it there. Grandma always had special treats at her house. Growing up in our home with two other siblings meant special foods and treats were doled out sparingly. Grandma's was a different story. Food was good and Grandma always was a soft touch. In fact, my Grandma was one of the most generous people I knew. She always greased us kids with money and sweets. It always was fun to visit or have a visit from my Grandma Armstrong. Her first name was Emma, and she is the second hero I will talk about. Emma will never be as famous as other heroes we know, but to those who knew her, she was a saint. One afternoon, I came to Grandma's sporting my Unicef box. Each Halloween, our school gave the kids Unicef boxes to carry with us when we went trick-or-treating for candy. The neighborhood kids would collect this change and the school would donate the money to Unicef in support of their various causes. When I asked Grandma for her support, she went to her purse and took out her pocket book. She took one shiny quarter and dropped it in my box. Now I have to tell you I was surprised. Grandma was the one person I thought I could count on to bolster the donations. I thought at least a fiver from Grandma. Being young and honest as kids are most times, I looked up at her and said, "Grandma, that's only a quarter. How can we help with only a quarter?" She told me something I will remember for life. She sat me down and said to me, "Son, if everybody put in a quarter, most of the world's charities would want for nothing." I learned about giving from Grandma Emma.

She always gave. She gave to anyone and everyone who asked and many who didn't ask. She used to do something special at Christmas time that only a few people ever learned about. She gave in many ways and kept it a secret. Today, her children, her grandchildren, and her great grandchildren, carry on her values and generosity. Already, her legacy has carried to the fourth generation.

When Emma Armstrong died, the entire town of Midland, Ontario showed up. Not because she was wealthy, or because she was "important." They turned out to respect one of the most caring, loving and generous people that God ever graced our world with. Grandma taught me the power of 25 cents. Today, I think that if there was an Emma in every town, we'd live in a much more loving world.

To me, being a hero in the age of celebrities is about quietly contributing and giving to our charities of choice. It's about living with a grateful heart and a willing spirit, sharing with others. After all, what pleasure is there in hoarding wealth or success? The pleasure is the sharing. I not only believe that charity and sharing is important. I believe it is essential to one's success. I know very few long-term success stories that do not include a regiment of giving. I believe the idea of charity needs to begin in our communities, with our businesses leading the way. This then continues to our schools, our churches, and civic clubs and organizations, which allow us to teach our children through our own example. It is necessary for them to take part in others' lives by giving something of themselves. It is this kind of thinking that builds heroes in an age of celebrities. I also believe that if possible, your giving be humble, not grandiose. Is your gift for them or for you? This humbling exercise will keep a glow in your heart. It did for the people I write about and it certainly has enriched my life.

I want to challenge you to do something an old recovering alcoholic taught me years ago. I came to my friend one day and began to lament over my personal tragedies and sorrows as I spilled my guts. I went over in detail all the things that were going wrong in my life. For more than 30 minutes, he listened quietly as I continued my verbal diarrhea. When I was done, I asked him what he thought. He told me my problem was that I was a selfish, self-centered whiner and that I needed to get outside of myself in order to understand true gratitude. He told me that my problems where inside my head and that I was wallowing in self pity. He had the cure, if I was interested. He told me to be ready to go at seven that night. I was a little perturbed at his forward nature, but respected his opinion a great deal; I agreed to go along with his plan.

Seven o'clock rolled around and sure enough, my friend was on time. I traveled in his car as we began to weave our way down into the belly of the place that I knew all too well just a few short years earlier. He parked his car in a seedy part of skid row and told me to follow him. I did, and soon I found myself waiting for the doors to open at our local alcohol and drug detox facility. Once inside, he leaned over and told me that to help myself, I must help others. That night, my friend taught me a valuable lesson. He taught me that no matter how bad I think I've got it, there's always someone less fortunate. He taught me that to stay grateful, you need to stay connected with other people. He also taught me that giving was the best way to get perspective on my own personal troubles.

That night, my friend asked me to share my experience with the men in detox. I shared how at one time, my life was ruined and I had to start again from nothing. I had been desperate, destitute and hopeless, but a miracle of recovery happened to me and I was certain it could happen for them. After the meeting, many of the guys thanked me for my time and my story. They told me it was inspiring and that it helped them. The feeling I had leaving that place was one of utter gratitude and joy. How could I have been so selfish and self absorbed? This lesson had such a profound effect on me that I committed to doing this work on a regular basis. In fact, this exercise in giving led me to becoming a professional speaker many years later.

After the meeting, I thanked my friend for what he had taught me. You see, as I was helping these men in detox, I was being helped. My life was put into focus and I gained the perspective I needed to continue with my struggles. The load seemed somehow lighter.

My wise old friend told me that if I wanted to continue feeling grateful, I needed to do this type of thing on a regular basis. He said to me that for the next 90 days, he wanted me to commit one act of random kindness each week, toward a person or group. The only criteria was that I had to do it in secret and I could only help people that had no way of helping me in return, hence creating an environment totally conducive to the essence of true charity.

I won't tell you what I did, but after only four weeks, I was hooked. Today, I so enjoy hunting for opportunities to exercise this spiritual activity. It has enriched my life in ways I can't describe. I was touched when I watched the movie, "Pay It Forward" with Haley Joel Osmond and Kevin Spacey. That movie really spoke to me about the impact one can make. How many apples are in your seed?

From that initial meeting at the detox facility, I went on to continue allocating time to speak to others in need. I began to speak in treatment centers, recovery houses, hospitals, prisons and high schools. It was on this path that I found my true passion. I love to watch people being moved by a great speaker. As a student of motivational change, I have witnessed some of the greatest speakers reach in and touch people's hearts. When I began working with people getting honest and sharing my journey, warts and all, I received this overwhelming love returning back to me. I knew it was what I wanted to do. It is from this seed-planting exercise that my whole world evolved and opened up.

Today, I find it amusing to hear my speaking colleagues talk about a particularly hard audience they had to address. I chuckle when I think about where I first got started. Talking to prison inmates, detoxifying drug addicts and teenagers in high schools. You think you have a tough audience — bring it on!

After my experience speaking with addicts and alcoholics, I decided I wanted to do more prevention education. I enjoy working with people in recovery and I feel I always will, but something in me said, "What if we could prevent a child from addiction or alcoholism?" I began my research work with my good friend, Chan Ramcharan. We looked into what kind of preventive curriculum was available for youth. We discovered there were lots of great programs from an intellectual point of view. We also discovered many programs from an "educational" or "knowledge" base being delivered. What we did not see was a program being delivered from a direct honest or emotional point of view. We wanted to create "reality based" education. Our theory was this: Get them to feel and we can change the way they think. We were right!!

On Feb. 9th 1999, we founded The Courage to Change Foundation. A society dedicated to educating youth on Drug and Alcohol abuse. It took us a year to refine our program, but when we were done, we had a Web site, a sound system, and a powerful, reality based program using multimedia, music and vivid large screen imagery to drive home a message that needs to be told. Our program is called "Don't Buy the Lie About Getting High."

What was different about what we did? We approached students by first respecting them and talking honestly. I told them I wasn't a cop, I wasn't a teacher, I didn't work for the school board and I wasn't being paid to be there. Then I told my story of how I started using drugs at the age of nine and managed to quit when I was 24. I talked about all the lies that led to my life of despair and then displayed pictures of friends of mine who did not make it.

What works about our program is our honesty, and the way we tell kids the exact   truth about what messing with drugs and alcohol could — and would — get them. All we are trying to do is plant some seeds. I have a little prayer I say before I begin any school event. I ask God to let just one kid hear the message that day. If just one kid hears the message, then all my pain and degradation will have meant something. I'm not sure how many lives we have effected, but in the last three years, I do know that I have spoken to more than 60,000 young people in British Columbia at more than 50 high schools. Each school told us that it was one of the most impacting programs they've ever had.

What's funny about this work is, if you had told me five years ago I would be working with youth, I would have told you that you were nuts. I hated kids. They bugged me. They had bizarre hairstyles, they listened to terrible music, and they dressed in clothes that were falling off their backsides. They terrorized the neighborhoods on their wheelie-boards. They were loud and obnoxious. They had attitudes and smart mouths, and I believed them to be a bunch of no good punks. And yet, through all my reservations and shortcomings, they took *me* at face value. An ex-junkie skid row bum was OK by them. They taught me that they were people with incredibly hard decisions to face each day. Decisions that my generation and that before me have no comprehension of. I learned that I was reading into the youth of today the kind of kid I was, not what they really are. As these young people and I connected, I learned to really dig them. In fact, I would rather spend an afternoon hanging out with a group of young people hungry for knowledge, than sitting in a stuffy boardroom making business decisions.

What happened in one of these events touched my heart. There was a young girl from Mission BC who had died from a drug overdose. She was 17 years old. Her mother was at one of my events, so I decided to dedicate the presentation to her memory. When I was done, the mother approached me and told me how much it meant to her to have someone honor her child in the name of prevention. Later that week, I was in my office when a package arrived. Inside were more than 50 letters from students telling me I made a difference at their school. That kids were reciting the phrase, "Don't Buy the Lie about Getting High" in the hallways and school cafeteria. In their letters, they told me how I had changed the way they thought about drugs and booze. They told me to keep telling my story to other kids. They told me the message reached their heads and their hearts. They told me I planted a seed!

I do this work not for glory or praise. In fact, I don't even like telling you about it but I need to make my point. I know that my life often has nothing to do with me. That some days I'm simply here to serve others and do my Father's will. I keep going by asking, seeking and knocking, not looking for reward. And then there are days when I'm surprised and delighted when someone says to me, "Your story really counted to us. Keep it up!"

Today, as a professional speaker traveling around the world talking to different audiences on inspiration, leadership and change, I still find time to connect with local schools. I always try to do a local school presentation the same day or trip I am addressing a convention or association dinner. Some events encourage families to attend. When this happens, I offer my youth service program without charge.

What makes a hero? Usually selflessness, generosity, and a soft and caring spirit are evident when you are in the presence of a hero. One of the people I look up to as a speaker, mentor and role model is Vancouver's Peter Legge. Peter is the CEO of the largest publishing company in Western Canada. He is recognized the world over for his masterful skill as a professional speaker and he currently holds just about every award known by the National Speakers Association and The Canadian Association of Professional Speakers. Peter is the kind of guy who gives often. He is out there making a difference in business and in the community. Last month, I had the pleasure of hearing Peter speak. I never get tired listening to a great speaker, especially when they talk

about truth. Peter is a guy that gives so much to his world
that his success and stature in the community is high. In his
office is a pile of the prestigious awards this man has been
given. I'm grateful for men like Peter Legge, who have paved
the way for the younger generation of business people and
professional speakers. His messages on balance and family are
my favorite. He truly is a profile and testament to good old
fashion ethics and personal integrity.

Now you may say, oh sure Joe, he wrote the forward to your
book, you ought to speak well of the man. Yes, I am grateful
for Peter's help, but not for those reasons. I watched Peter
from a distance for more than three years before I introduced
myself to him. He walked the talk and showed me that being
a hero is not just hammering out a great speech or writing a
fat cheque to charity. It means much more than that. Life isn't
about getting it right when people are looking… it's about
living what you believe. It's about being real all the time.

When I was ready to meet with Peter, I sent him an email
talking about my admiration of his career. I said I would very
much like to meet with him for a few minutes and discuss
business and this book you're reading now. I called his
assistant, Janice Maxell (who is a gem of a woman in her own
right), and after some juggling, she managed to find time in
Peter's busy schedule. The day arrived and I was escorted into
Peter's corner office at Canada Wide Magazines. I was about
to meet a guy I respect immensely. In his hands, Peter had the
power to liberate me and my hopes and dreams or with a few
short words, crush them. We chatted as I did most of the
talking for about 10 minutes. I had little time and needed to
disclose in a direct, but somehow discrete manner, my story.
When I was done sharing, Peter didn't flinch. In fact, he began
to encourage me and told me my story had a place on the
professional platform. He then told me other pieces of

wisdom that I have held close. When it was all said and done, Peter, one the busiest guys in Western Canada, said that he would help — even after I had told him who I was and where I came from. Imagine that!

I left that meeting on a real high. Since his encouragement, I have met other great people who have encouraged my efforts. I met Charles "Tremendous" Jones, Lesra Martin, Rick Hansen, and Silken Laumann, all of whom have encouraged and cheered me on. To all who played a role helping me, I am grateful. I did not make it alone to where I am. Nobody does it alone. I am so grateful for the help of others planting a seed in me.

Many years ago, I met a fellow named Ian. Ian, by today's standards, has all the trappings of success. He has a nice car, a beautiful home, a lovely wife and wonderful well-balanced children. He owns a great company and by society's standards, Ian is very successful. But life for Ian had not always been so good. In fact, Ian had a similar story as mine. As a young person, he got into a bunch of trouble and found himself heading toward grave danger when something happened and he decided to change. Fortunately, for Ian, he caught himself before too much damage had been done.

As a teen, Ian used to hang out downtown with a rough crowd and began to do drugs and party at the age of 14. By the time he was 16, he had been in trouble with the law, his grades had deteriorated and he found himself on the outs with his parents more often than not. He hung around on the streets and only went home when he needed fresh clothes and a good sleep. Ian was well on his way to being a street kid if something didn't change.

When Ian hung out downtown, he often frequented the local youth drop-in center where he could get food and other resources. A lot of his buddies used this place as a hang out or place to use a phone or do their laundry. While at the center one day, Ian met a caseworker named Bob. Bob was a really kind old guy who cared and helped a lot of young people who came into the center. One afternoon, Bob and Ian were talking when Bob asked how things were going. Ian was honest and told him how it was at home and at school. Bob listened without judgment and asked him what he thought the smart thing to do might be. Ian told him he knew he was in for trouble, but felt he just couldn't go back to his parents. He felt he was beyond reconciliation.

Bob shared with Ian some opinions parents have. How he thought Ian's parents would welcome him back home. How they ultimately wanted success for him and that they loved him no matter what. Ian listened and later that week, he went home and sorted things out with his folks and his school. From there, he went on to become the success he is today.

A few years passed, and Ian found out his old friend Bob had passed away. He began to think back to the time Bob had shared his wisdom with him and how it had been a turning point in his life. He began to feel tremendous gratitude and decided it was time for him to give to the community the way Bob had given to him. Ian went down on Saturday morning and volunteered at the drop-in center. He decided that from now on, he was going to give back to the community in this special way. One reason for doing so was as a tribute to Bob and the other was to see if through teen mentorship, maybe he could make a difference like Bob. Maybe he could plant his seed and watch it grow like Bob had with him.

As the weeks went by, Ian got to know all the familiar faces from the downtown area. One young man he met was named Johnny. Johnny was a fireball of a young man. He was sharp-witted, funny, and was well liked by the staff and kids at the youth center. Anytime Johnny was in the center, you could always hear laughter and good cheer. What was dangerous about Johnny was his lifestyle. He was known to use drugs and hang around with an unsavory bunch of local street kids.

When Ian met Johnny, he was struck by how similar Johnny was to himself when he was that age. His sense of humor, his rebellious attitude toward his parents, school and the local police. Ian felt that they were kindred spirits and decided he was going to try and make a difference in Johnny's life. He was going to plant his seed.

One gray Saturday morning, theopportunity came. It had been raining for a few days and all the kids were coming in wet and cold. Johnny was no different. He dragged himself into the center around ten o'clock looking like a drowned rat. Ian noticed he looked really rough, as though the drugs and the streets were taking their toll. He also noticed that Johnny had lost quite a bit of weight. He approached Johnny and asked him if he'd like to go out for lunch and enjoy a hot meal. Johnny replied sarcastically, "Better fed than dead Fred," and off they went.

Around the corner from the center was a greasy spoon that served excellent cheeseburgers, so they found a booth and sat down. The restaurant was a throw back from the 50s, with traditional booths and a jukebox in the corner. They also complemented the décor with a traditional 50s-style menu. As Johnny sat on his side of the booth sipping his milkshake, Ian asked him how he was. He replied fine, but Ian knew he wasn't. Ian decided he'd share a little deeper and try and connect with Johnny. Ian shared what his life had been like before he turned it around. He talked about being off track and living a street lifestyle. Over the hour that followed, Ian shared all the good things in life. He talked about reconciling with his family. He talked about getting clean and sober. He talked about going back to school and looking to his future. Ian really poured it out for him that day, but something was missing in Johnny. He seemed to shrug off his advice and make light of what was going on for him. He told Ian it wasn't all that bad and that he'd be fine, he was just having a bad week.

After Ian shared with him everything he could think of, Johnny thanked him for lunch and left. As Ian sat alone in the booth, he knew that if Johnny didn't change things fast, something terrible was going to happen.

Two weeks later, Ian's premonition played out. He arrived to volunteer one Saturday morning and heard the news that Johnny had died from a drug overdose. Ian was sick with grief. He mulled over in his head the things he could possibly have said that may have changed Johnny's fate. He was so sad and torn apart at the news.

As the weeks, months and years passed, Ian never forgot about Johnny. In some small way, he felt as though he had failed him. That he hadn't done enough. Years passed and Ian went on to greater success in life and business, yet never stopped volunteering his time at the youth center. Although he was active, as a volunteer, something in him was lost when Johnny died.

More than 10 years passed, when one day, Ian was in a board meeting on the 17th floor of a prominent downtown office building. His company was involved in a large contract and this meeting was to bring everybody involved up-to-date on the new changes about to take place in the next quarter. In the meeting were people from marketing, finance, sales, advertising and the executive management board. When the meeting broke up, Ian packed up his things and found himself facing a window that looked down onto the youth center and he couldn't help thinking about Johnny.

As he turned around, he found himself facing a well-dressed young man who had just taken part in the meeting. He was the representative from advertising. The young man looked deep into Ian's eyes as if he were searching for something. Ian asked how he could help. The man said, "I've been looking for you for a very long time. Today, while listening to you speak, I recognized your voice." Ian said he didn't quite understand. The young man continued by saying, "A long time ago, you helped me get my life together." Ian searched his memory and said that he didn't remember this young man at all and that he must be mistaken.

The young man continued and asked Ian, "Do you remember a lunch meeting you had more than 10 years ago?" They were now staring out the window together as the young man pointed below, "You met with my friend, Johnny, in that restaurant down there and you told him about the good things in life. You talked about the importance of family, about staying in school and about staying off drugs." Ian was shocked and said, "Yes! Yes! I remember that meeting. I remember Johnny, I remember the conversation, but I don't remember you, how could I possibly have helped you?" The young man looked at Ian and said, "I was at the restaurant that day. I was sitting in the booth behind you. I heard your message and I followed your advice and went home that night. I got sober, went back to school, graduated from the university and now I have a successful career in advertising."

Ian was speechless. With tears streaming down his 40-something cheeks, he realized that his seed *had* been planted. The young man's name was Peter. The two locked shoulders and hugged. They stood there in silence sharing their spiritual moment.

That evening over dinner, Peter shared with Ian all the volunteer work that he was involved in and all the seeds he'd been planting. What Ian learned was, all those years when he thought he had failed Johnny, he had actually served Peter. His seed was firmly planted and was reaping bountiful fruit in many places.

How many apples are in a seed? That depends on you!

I had just finished telling this story at an event in Toronto. No sooner had the applause subsided and the meeting planner took stage to thank me for my inspirational message. When I was on my way down from the stage, a young man ran up to me and said, "Package for Mr. Roberts," and thrust it into my hands. I tucked it under my arm as I headed to the autograph table to shake hands, accept hugs and sign some books.

Later that evening, I was packing my things preparing to go home, when my curiosity got the best part of me. Sitting on the edge of the bed looking at this plainly wrapped square-sized package, I started unwrapping it. I was stunned to find what it contained.

It was my rose-colored prayer box. Remember the rose-colored prayer box? As I pulled all the wrapping off, I saw my original shoebox, the one my wife Jennifer had given me. It still had the old rose-colored paper, but looked like it had been on an incredible journey.

The corners were pretty banged up. The lid had a big scratch on it, but all in all, it was still the same prayer box. My mind began to race. Who was that messenger boy? How did my box travel from BC to Toronto? I threw that box in the air more than 18 months ago and it had gone up and completely disappeared. Why did it come back to me now? What did this mean? How could it be? Where had it been? In my frenzied state of confusion, I figured there was only way to find out.

I tore open the box expecting to find all the thoughts and worries I had put into it. Instead, I found one small piece of paper. Written on the note in perfect handcrafted calligraphy was this message:

The secrets you have been given
Your worries you need not fear
All that you need for today and tomorrow
Is staring back at you from your mirror
Live your life by your own declaration
Seeking solace and comfort above
Remember your wealth and your wisdom
Is to be shared with others in love
Courage is yours on this journey called life
Know that far will be not my eye
To love, guard, teach and to protect

Signed, your angel in disguise

the Beginning

For more information or to inquire about a speaking engagement call: 604-468-2190 or email *info@joeroberts.ca*

To find out about additional Joe Roberts books and products visit *www.joeroberts.ca*

Don't forget to sign up to our Profit From Adversity E-Newsletter and receive additional stories, special offers and discounts on upcoming publications.

About *the* Author

Joe Roberts is an expert on personal development and inspirational change. In 1989 he was living on the streets of Vancouver as a homeless skid row derelict. Today he is the CEO of Mindware Design Communications. He is a dramatic example of courage and determination.

When he speaks of improving lives, he speaks from personal experience. From his days on the streets of Vancouver to the stress and challenges of running a business during tough times, he draws on his real-life experience and teaches how anyone can tap into the unconquerable power of the human spirit and rise above adversity.

He is an internationally sought after professional speaker who motivates and inspires audiences with his "YES I CAN" attitude.

In his spare time he supports The Courage to Change Foundation, a society dedicated to youth drug prevention and education.

He is both a husband and father of one and enjoys his new home with Jennifer and Sarah in Coquitlam, BC.

Walk in the shoes of a former penniless drug addict. Learn the attitude and philosophy that changed one man's living hell into a classic Rags-to-Riches story of success. Enrich your next conference or convention with one of the most unique professional speakers on the circuit today.